The Essential Ninja Dual Zone Air Fryer Cookbook UK

Quick, Healthy and Affordable Recipes for Beginners incl. Side Dishes, Desserts and More

Elsie M. Flynn

Contents

Introduction

Getting to Know the Ninja Dual Zone Air Fryer

The duel zone is amongst my top 3 favourite air fryer units due to its versatility and ability to cook different food products simultaneously. Not to mention, at varying temperatures, varying times, and with varying cooking methods.

NOW THAT'S A LOT OF VARIATION!

For example, you could 'ROAST' some lamb chops at 180°C for 8 minutes, and 'BAKE' some potatoes at 200°C for 15 minutes.

At this current time, it costs less than £200 at a capacity of 7.6L. So between us, its reasonably priced and does not take up too much space in the kitchen.

The duel zone unit is 75% more energy efficient compared to more complex cooking appliances, so you could save a lot of money, especially with the current energy crises in the UK.

I really admire the duel zone unit for its ability to save so much time and effort, putting together top quality recipes that are 75% faster than fan ovens.

Weight gain and obesity being a major epidemic in the UK, the duel zone unit can cook food with 75% less fat than the original recipes, which could potentially scrape off a few hundred calories and support healthy weight management.

The duel zone unit has 6 unique cooking functions and 2 settings that I have highlighted below.

Once purchasing the dual zone air fryer, you will get:

- The air fryer unit
- 2 zone draws
- 2 crisper plates
- Basic manual

You also have the option to purchase separate attachments such as:

- Silicon air fryer liners
- Stainless steel skewers
- Air fryer oil brush
- Cake pans
- Air fryer liner paper
- Stainless steel rack
- Air fryer tongs
- Pizza pans
- Metal holder
- Egg bite moulds

In all honesty, these separate attachments are not necessary to put together your favourite meals, but are great accessories, especially if you are an air fryer fanatic.

Why I chose the Ninja Duel Zone Air Fryer?

At first, I brought the duel zone air fryer to jump on the 'hype train', little did I know that I would fall in love.

The duel zone air fryer is so easy to manoeuvre and efficient with time, yet cooks the perfect meals. I practically cook all of my meals using the air fryer, by utilising all 6 of its functions. The features I use the most are 'AIR FRY' 'ROAST', and 'REHEAT'.

To be honest, I have cooked many Sunday roast dinners and even Christmas dinners from the turkey, down to the apple sauce and gravy.

What I realised was that the energy bill had reduced significantly, and I felt much healthier and fitter after 3 months of using it.

I would certainly recommend the dual zone air fryer to all of my friends and family.

Main Features of The Ninja Dual Zone Air Fryer

'MAX CRISP'

The 'MAX CRISP' is a unique function of the duel zone. This function is similar to the 'AIR FRY' in that it apply the same cooking mechanism. In my personal experience I have only employed this function whilst cooking excessively frozen foods or crisps. This function differs in that it has a pre-set temperature of 240°C, which is the maximum temperature of the duel zone unit.

'AIR FRY'

'AIR FRY' is like the little brother of 'MAX CRISP', in the sense that it is typically employed to cook 'fry up' type of foods like fries, chicken tenders, battered fish, Kentucky, breaded fish fingers etc. The maximum temperature of this function is 210°C.

'ROAST'

The 'ROAST' function is another great incorporation of the duel zone unit. We all love our Sunday roast, and this unique function allows us to put together many of our favourite pieces like whole chicken and roast vegetables. The maximum temperature of this function is 210°C, which is perfect for roasting.

'REHEAT'

Typically, you would utilise the 'REHEAT' function whilst warming up foods that have already been cooked. For example, I love reheating 'yesterday's Sheppard's pie' to revive the flavours and textures. The 'REHEAT' function is set to 170°C which is perfect for most refrigerated foods.

'DEHYDRATE'

'DEHYDRATE' is another unique function of air fryers. As the name suggests, it allows you to dehydrate food products. I absolutely love this function to dry sliced fruit like oranges and lemons that are great for cocktail accessories. The temperature on this function starts from 40°C, which would typically be applied for hours to remove the moisture from foods.

'BAKE'

We all know those baking fanatics who have the tastiest recipe for cakes, pastries, and brownies. The 'BAKE' function on the ninja duel unit is perfect for these tasty treats. Even if you aren't an

experienced Baker, the duel zone unit will do hard work, all you need to do, is put together the ingredients of your favourite treat from our recipe book. Personally, this function allows me to bake meats just the way I like it. Like most of the other functions the maximum temperature for 'BAKE' is 210°.

'SYNC'

SYNC allows you to apply two different functions at varying cooking times on the food content in each duel zone draw. Let's say you want to put together a burger and fries. You may want to apply 'ROAST' at 180°C for 10 minutes to the zone 1 draws (burger meat) and 'AIR FRY' at 200°C for 12 minutes to the zone 2 draw (fries). You would then press 'START/STOP' and let the duel zone do its magic.

The duel zone will finish cooking foods at the same time, as it will initiate the draw with the longest cooking duration, and start cooking the content within the second draw as soon as the times are matched.

'MATCH'

This setting allows you to cook the food content into both zone draws at the same time. Let's say you want to cook a big batch of French fries, you could fill up the zone draws and select 'AIR FRY' at 200°C for 12 minutes, then press 'MATCH' followed by 'START/STOP'.

The Advantages Of The Ninja Dual Zone Air Fryer

Versatility

As mentioned in the previous section, the duel zone is very versatile with 6 different cooking functions, 2 different settings, and temperatures from 40°– 240°C.

Not to forget, it allows you to cook two different food products simultaneously, without having to constantly look over them.

Reliability

The duel zone has a years guarantee, but in my experience it has longer even with multiple uses per day.

Furthermore, the attachments and base itself is sturdy, so I would not expect it to crack or break that easily.

Cook Healthier Alternatives

Without delving into too much detail, dietary fat is the most caloric dense macronutrient with 9Kcal per gram.

That being said, consuming high fat foods on a regular basis increases the risk of becoming chronically overweight or obese, with subsequent health decrement like heart disease and diabetes.

The duel zone unit possesses fryer like functions, that would normally require us to saturate foods in fatty oils.

Could you imagine 'air frying' the perfect coated fish and chips with practically no oil, certainly fewer calories than the local chippi.

YOU COULD SAY THE DUEL ZONE IS MODERN DAY SORCERY! (**LOL**).

Great Option For Reheating Food

Jokes aside, the duel zone unit has the capability of rejuvenating last nights food tasting fresh.

Have you ever tied Reheating 'last night's leftovers' in the microwave? The texture is like cardboard right?

Well, by simply placing the food content in the duel zone and selecting the 'REHEAT' at 170°C for 5-7 minutes will have your food tasting fresh.

Cook Advanced Meals

The Duel Zone allows you to put together advanced meals that otherwise would only be seen in a 'chef Gordon's Kitchen'.

For example, with the touch a few buttons, you could bake yourself the most magnificent chocolate birthday cake on the block.

Not Restricted To Specific Groups

We love the fact that there are no restrictions to who can and can not use the duel zone.

You could be the 'average Joey' who only knows how to toast some bread, or a 'master chef Oliver' who can cook the perfect Fugu puffer pie.

Very Easy to Clean

Unlike other air fryer models, the duel zone is very easy to clean and all you require is a:

- Kitchen sponge
- Washing up solution
- Warm running tap
- Stainless steel scourer (optional)
- Damp cloth

I have outlined 7 in depth steps below and 3 additional tips and tricks

The Ninja Duel Zone Care And Cleaning Tips

It's very common to use the Duel zone on a daily basis, causing a build up of grease and old food residue. For this reason, it is crucial to give your unit a good clean on a regular basis. Let's face it, the last thing we want is last week's bread crumbs in our freshly cooked Sheppard's pie.

I have highlighted our experts step-by-step 'how to' guide on cleaning your duel zone unit.

1. Start by removing the zone draws and the crisper plates, then brush out any crumbs from the main unit.
2. Using a damp cloth, clean the main unit, but ensure that the plugs are removed
3. Using hot water from a running tap, wash the internal compartment of the zone draws and remove the leftover food content
4. Scrape the dry grease and residue using a kitchen sponge and washing up liquid, then wash it off via the warm running water
5. Dry the draws using a cloth and put them aside
6. Scrub the crisper plates using a stainless steel scourer or sponge and washing up liquid, whilst running them under warm water
7. Dry the crisper plates using a cloth and put them aside

Additional Tips And Tricks

We have provided some additional tips and tricks, for you to get a better idea of how to clean and maintain your duel zone draw.

1. Clean the duel zone after every use, or the very least after 2-3 uses
2. Clean the zone draws as soon as possible if you are cooking greasy foods such as sausages, burgers, steaks, chops etc.
3. If you are hand cleaning the duel zone

attachments, be sure to use a good grease removing solution.

Real User Reviews

'As a 20-year old in my first apartment, this was the best Xmas gift!!!'

Amanda. M

'I like this airfryer so much, we just got it last week and it's very convenient and you can't beat the price '

Pamela. S

'Easy to use good size 2 deep pans drawers cook in no time saves mega on fuel bill well worth money would recommend to anybody who is looking for an air fryer '

Terence. F

'Purchased this for myself a couple of months ago and wasnt really sure if I would use it, but after 2 months I wouldn't be without it. Not used my electric oven since! This produce has a range of cooking options and temperatures for all kinds of food. It can do everything your oven does (and more) for a fraction of the price. I was so impressed I ordered another two for my daughters '

Julie. M

Frequently Asked Questions

Q1: 'Can you use foil in the duel zone air fryer?'

A1: There is no restriction to foil, in fact with some recipes it is essential that you use foil

Q2: 'What functions can I use to cook fries?'

A2: The most common employed function for food that would be traditionally fried, would be the 'AIR FRY' alternative

Q3: 'How many functions does the duel zone have air fryer have?'

A3: The duel zone has 6 unique functions which include;

- MAX CHRISP
- AIR FRY
- ROAST
- REHEAT
- DEHYDRATE
- BAKE

Q4: 'What is the minimum and maximum temperature of the duel zone?'

A4:The lowest temperature is 40°C that is specific to the 'DEHYDRATE' function and 240°C which can only be applied by 'MAX CRISP'. The 'REHEAT' function max temperature is 170°C and the remainder 3 functions ('ROAST' 'BAKE' 'AIR FRY') go up to 210°C

Q5: 'Why do I keep hearing that the duel zone air fryer is healthier than traditional cooking methods?'

A5: It's an alternative that requires much less oil. Oil contains fat and fat is very high in calories, thereby the duel zone air fryer can cook up tasty meals and snacks at lower calories. In turn, this can help maintain energy balance, prevent weight gain, and any associated illnesses.

Q6: 'Are there any limitations to the duel zone air fryer?'

A6: The only limitations I can see is that you would need to clean it regularly. But then again you'll also need to clean gas cookers and ovens after, which in more difficult to clean in my opinion

Q7: 'What makes the duel zone air fryer a better alternative to traditional cooking appliances?'

A7: Firstly the duel zone is much cheaper to purchase. Secondly, it is a lot smaller to store and maintain. Thirdly, you can cook exactly the same meals, simpler and quicker. Fourthly, the meals can be a lot 'healthier'. Lastly, the duel zone unit uses less energy.

Q8: 'How would you compare the duel zone air fryer to the microwave for reheating food?'

A8: In my personal experience the duel zone air fryer revives a high quality flavours and textures, whereas the microwave makes a lot of foods soggy. The only benefit of using the microwave is that it's a lot more time efficient with heating food.

Q9: 'Do you need to Preheat the duel zone air fryer?'

A9: You certainly do! Usually you will need to heat the unit to the temperature that you will cook your food. The duration of preheating can be anywhere from 3-10 minutes

Q10: 'Why does this air fryer have 2 compartments?'

A10: You could either use the compartments to cook lots of food in bulk, or cook a variety of foods at one time

Q11: 'Can you use washing up liquid and water to clean the main unit of the duel zone air fryer?

A11: NO! You must never use water on the internal units of the duel zone air fryer, as it may cause damage

Q12: 'Is the duel zone air fryer the best model?'

A12: in my opinion it's amongst the best 3, as it has so many applications. The only thing that lets it down for me is that it does not have a 'pressure-cook' 'sear' 'sauté' 'steam' or 'slow cook' functions

Q13: 'How can I cook a chicken breast using the duel zone air fryer?'

A13: There here are many ways in which you could cook your chicken breast via the duel zone air fryer. You can 'BAKE' or 'ROAST' which differ in terms of texture. Another method of cooking your chicken breast could be 'AIR FRY' but you may want to find a recipe that coats your chicken breast with breadcrumbs.

Q14: 'Can you use silicon bakeware in the duel zone air fryer, or will it melt?'

A14: You can indeed use silicon bakeware. Even if we applied the duel zones maximum 240°C temperature, it is not high enough to melt such elements. Just out of interest, the melting point for silicon is 1414°C, which is almost 1/3 the temperature of the sun.

Q15: 'Can I use duel air fryer as a microwave?'

A15: The duel air fryer and microwave differentiate greatly. If you mean 'can I warm my food up in the duel air fryer', you absolutely can! But I warn you, the food content will warm to a much better quality compared to the micro *HaHaHa*

Breakfast Burritos

Prep time : 20 mins
Cook time: 15 mins
Serves 4

Ingredients

- 1 medium potato
- 1 tablespoon oil
- 6 flour tortillas
- 4 eggs
- 32 ml milk, preferably whole milk
- 128 ml shredded cheddar cheese
- 1 teaspoon salt, and more to taste
- 1/2 teaspoon pepper, and more to taste
- 225 g raw breakfast sausage

Preparation Instructions :

1. Your Ninja Foodi air fryer should be preheated to 400 degrees.Cut your potatoes into 1/2-inch cubes, then season with salt, pepper, and oil. The potatoes should be placed in the air fryer and cooked for around 8 minutes before being removed and left aside.
2. While doing so, fry the sausage by breaking it into crumbs in a pan over medium heat. Keep the fat in the skillet after removing and setting aside.
3. In a bowl, combine the eggs, milk, and salt & pepper to taste. Pour this mixture into the heated pan with the sausage fat. Eggs should be scrambled until they become fluffy. Take out of the skillet, then set it aside.
4. In a bowl, mix the scrambled eggs, cooked potatoes, cooked sausage, and cheddar cheese.
5. Six tortillas should be filled evenly with the mixture, then sealed. A toothpick can be used to hold them shut.
6. Place the burritos in the air fryer after spraying with oil. Cook for 7 to 8 minutes at 380 degrees, spraying and turning the burrito halfway through.
7. Breakfast burritos should be taken out of the air fryer and served.

Pancakes

Prep time : 5 mins
Cook time: 36 mins
Serves 5-6

Ingredients

- 192 g all-purpose flour
- ¼ teaspoon kosher salt
- 1 large egg
- 192 g buttermilk (or regular milk)
- 1 ½ teaspoons baking powder
- 2-3 teaspoons granulated sugar
- 2 tablespoons unsalted butter, melted and slightly cooled

Preparation Instructions :

1. Combine the flour, baking soda, sugar, and salt in a mixing basin. After combining with a whisk, make a well in the center of the dry ingredients.
2. Beat the egg, whisk in the milk, and then add the melted butter to a different bowl.
3. Leave a few lumps left when you gently whisk the wet mixture into the wet mixture to just incorporate it.
4. The batter should rest for five minutes. In the meantime, place a 6-inch cake pan inside the basket of your air fryer, close it, and preheat it to 360 degrees F.
5. Spray the cake pan liberally with cooking spray before turning on the air fryer. A 64 ml of batter should be dropped into the cake pan using an ice cream scoop, and the remaining batter should be smoothed out to the pan's sides using a rubber spatula.
6. No need to flip the pancakes; air fried for 6 to 8 minutes until golden brown. Continue with the remaining batter, cooking the pancakes as before, and storing them on a baking sheet in a 200°F oven until ready to serve.

Potato Pancakes

Prep time : 10 mins
Cook time: 9 mins
Serves 4-6

Ingredients

- 750 g of shredded hash browns
- 1 teaspoon of paprika
- Salt and pepper to taste
- 32 ml of all purpose flour
- 1 egg
- 2-3 green onions
- 1 teaspoon of garlic

Preparation Instructions :

1. In a large bowl, combine the hash browns that have been shredded, the garlic, paprika, salt,

pepper, flour, and egg.

2. Only the green portion of your green onions should be chopped, and then mix them in with the other ingredients.

3. Turn on the Ninja foodi air fryer and heat it to 370 degrees.

4. Make your pancakes while it's cooking up. Spooned the mixture into a measuring cup with a 32 ml capacity. Shook it out after that, and it took the shape of a measuring cup. To shape the mixture into a pancake, merely applied pressure. Spray your basket's bottom liberally once your air fryer is ready. The basket should include your potato cakes. Avoid packing it too tightly because you'll need space to rotate them halfway through the cooking process.

5. After 4 minutes, turn the food. Your potato pancakes should cook for a further 4-5 minutes after being sprayed on top.

6. If preferred, top with more green onions and sour cream before serving.

Air Fryer Bacon and Egg Cups

Prep time : 10 mins
Cook time: 10 mins
Serves 6

Ingredients
- 3 slices bacon, sliced in half
- Diced bell pepper, optional
- 6 large eggs
- Salt and pepper, optional

Preparation Instructions :
1. Bacon strips should be cut in half. Half a piece of bacon is placed into each wrapper.
2. Use the bacon as support for the runny egg as you carefully break one inside each wrapper.
3. Add salt, pepper, and chopped peppers, to taste.
4. Be cautious not to knock any of the cups over when you gently close the air fryer basket. 10 minutes of cooking at 330°. Depending on your egg preferences, the timing will change. You should start with 8 minutes if you want your eggs over-medium. Egg yolks will be overcooked after ten minutes.
5. Carefully remove the baked egg cups after they are done to your preference. They'll be really warm. Add any desired toppings, such as green onions.

Cheesy Baked Eggs

Prep time : 4 mins
Cook time: 16 mins
Serves 2

Ingredients

- 4 large Eggs
- 56 g Smoked gouda, chopped
- Everything bagel seasoning
- Kosher salt and pepper to taste

Preparation Instructions :

1. Each ramekin should be sprayed with cooking spray inside. Each ramekin should contain 2 eggs and 28 g of gouda that has been diced. To taste, add salt and pepper. Sprinkle your everything bagel seasoning on top of each ramekin
2. Each ramekin should be put into the Ninja foodi air fryer basket. Cook for 16 minutes at 400F, or until eggs are fully cooked. Serve.

Air Fryer Blueberry Bread

Prep time : 5 mins
Cook time: 30 mins
Serves 15 slices

Ingredients

- 128 ML of milk
- 384 g of bisquick
- 32 g of protein powder
- 3 eggs
- 193 g of frozen blueberries

Preparation Instructions :

1. All ingredients should be well mixed. It will be a thick mixture.
2. Place in a loaf pan and air fry for 30 minutes at 350 degrees.
3. Insert a toothpick to test the doneness of the bread; it should come out clean.

White chocolate and raspberry scones

Prep time : 10 mins
Cook time: 12 mins
Serves 12

Ingredients

- 300g self-raising flour
- 40g butter, chopped
- 60g white chocolate, chopped

- 185ml milk, plus 1 tbsp extra
- 60g frozen raspberries
- Whipped cream, to serve
- Icing sugar, to dust

Preparation Instructions :

1. Fill a big bowl with the flour. Rub the butter into the flour with your hands until it resembles fine breadcrumbs. Add the white chocolate and stir. Make a well in the middle.
2. Mixture of flour and milk should be added. Stir with a flat-bladed knife until almost mixed. Gently whisk in the raspberries after adding them. on a surface that has been gently dusted with flour. The dough should be combined and gently worked until just smooth.
3. Dough is pressed into a disc that is 2 cm thick. Cut 12 rounds from the dough using a round pastry cutter with a diameter of 5 cm, trying to make the scones as close together as you can.
4. Use baking paper to line the Ninja Foodi air fryer. To allow air to flow, make a few small holes in the paper with a little knife. Gently group the scones in the air fryer and gently milk the tops (depending on the size of your air fryer, you may have to do this in 2 batches).
5. The scones should be brown and risen after 12 minutes in the oven at 180°C.

Air fryer Cheese and bacon scones

Prep time : 10 mins
Cook time: 15 mins
Serves 9

Ingredients

- 300g plain flour
- 30g butter, chopped
- 225ml milk, plus 1 tbsp extra to brush
- 80g grated tasty cheese
- 2 shortcut bacon rashers, finely chopped

Preparation Instructions :

1. The flour should be put in a big bowl. Rub the butter (30g butter, diced) into the flour using your hands until it resembles fine breadcrumbs. Pour the milk into the well you've created in the center. Stir the dough with a flat-bladed knife until it just comes together.
2. Lay the dough out on a surface that has been lightly dusted with flour. The dough should be combined and gently worked until just smooth. Disc the dough out to a thickness of 2 cm. Cut 9 rounds from the dough using a 6.5 cm round cutter, Make sure to cut the scones as closely together as you can.
3. Trim the baking paper to exactly fit the base of Ninja Foodi air fryer basket. To allow the air to flow, make a few small holes in the paper with a little knife. Place the scones on the paper

so that they barely touch, then delicately brush the tops with more milk.

4. Cook scones for 10 minutes at 180°C, or until they have risen and turned golden. Open the drawer and turn off the air fryer. Sprinkle the scones with the cheese and bacon mixture.
5. Cook for a further 5 minutes, or until the bacon is crispy and the cheese has melted.

Air fryer cheese bread puffs

Prep time : 20 mins
Cook time: 1h 15mins
makes 32

Ingredients

- 250ml milk
- 125ml vegetable oil
- 300g tapioca flour
- 2 eggs
- 70g finely grated parmesan cheese

Preparation Instructions :

1. In a saucepan, boil the milk and oil over medium heat for 2 minutes, or until the milk simmers. Add the flour and blend by stirring. Mixture should be transferred to a stand mixer's bowl. Beat for two minutes, or until smooth and slightly chilled.
2. One at a time, beat thoroughly after each addition before adding the eggs. Just mix the cheese after adding it. Make balls out of tablespoons of batter using wet hands.
3. Baking paper should be trimmed to suit the base of Ninja foodi air fryer basket. Place the balls on the baking paper 5 cm apart. 15 minutes of cooking at 180°C or until golden and puffy. the remaining balls, then repeat. Serve.

Apple and custard crumble rolls

Prep time : 15 mins
Cook time: 10 mins
makes 6

Ingredients

- 240g apple slices pie fruit
- 45g sultanas
- 1/2 tsp ground cinnamon
- 6 frozen spring roll wrappers, thawed
- 120g bought thick vanilla custard, plus extra, to serve
- 3 McVitie's Digestives The Original biscuits, finely chopped

- 25g rolled oats
- Cinnamon sugar, to serve

Preparation Instructions :

1. In a medium bowl, mix the apple, sultanas, and cinnamon.
2. Place 1 spring roll wrapper on a clear work area with the corner facing you. Just below the center of the wrapper, place one-sixth of the apple mixture. Apply custard with a brush on the wrapping. the sides in. To envelop the filling, roll up. Repeat to create a total of 6 rolls. Apply remaining custard to rolls.
3. On a plate, mix the oats and biscuits by stirring. One at a time, dip rolls in the oat mixture.
4. Spray oil on the Ninja foodi air fryer's basket. Spray oil on rolls before placing them in the air fryer basket. For 6-7 minutes or until golden and crisp, air fried at 200°C. Onto a serving platter after transfer.
5. Sprinkle cinnamon sugar on the rolls. Extra custard should be served.

Tropical French toast

Prep time : 10 mins
Cook time: 20 mins
serves 4

Ingredients

- 1 papaya
- 2 bananas
- 60ml almond milk
- 1/2 tsp ground cinnamon
- 4 eggs, lightly whisked
- 8 sourdough bread slices
- 250g natural yoghurt
- Fresh mint leaves, to serve

Preparation Instructions :

1. Trim the papaya's two ends. To peel vegetables, use a vegetable peeler. Reduce in half. scrape out the seeds. One half should be chopped coarsely and put in a blender. Set aside the remaining half.
2. Blend banana, almond milk, and cinnamon in a blender until well combined.
3. In a bowl, put the eggs. Stir the 125ml of papaya mixture in before adding it. Allow the excess to trickle back into the bowl as you dip two pieces of bread into the egg mixture. Spray oil on the air fryer basket. the air fryer basket with the bread that has been coated. Five minutes of air frying at 200C. Use the remaining bread and egg mixture in the same way.
4. In the meantime, blend the yoghurt with the 125ml of papaya mixture in a dish by stirring.

The remaining papaya should be cut in half. Slice the first half crosswise. Finely chop remaining papaya half.

5. On a serving platter, put a piece of french toast. Add some papaya and yoghurt mixture on top with a tablespoon. Add a second slice of french toast, some of the yoghurt mixture, then some of the papaya mixture on top. Add the finely chopped and sliced papaya on top. Repetition is necessary with the remaining bread, yoghurt mixture, papaya combination, and sliced and diced papaya. To serve, sprinkling mint leaves.

Air fryer coccoli

Prep time : 1h 15mins
Cook time: 20 mins
makes 16

Ingredients

- 185ml warm water
- 7g sachet dried yeast
- 1 tsp salt
- Pinch of caster sugar
- 300g plain flour
- 2 tbsp olive oil, plus extra to grease and drizzle
- Fresh ricotta, to serve
- Prosciutto slices, coarsely torn, to serve

Preparation Instructions :

1. Salt, sugar, yeast, and water are all combined in a container. Until the yeast dissolves, whisk. Set aside till foamy after 5 minutes.
2. Make a well in the center of a big bowl of flour. Use a wooden spoon to whisk the oil and yeast mixture together after adding them both. The dough should be mixed together with clean hands. After turning the dough onto a lightly dusted surface, knead for 5 minutes, or until it is smooth and elastic.
3. Grease a dish very lightly. Put the dough in the bowl, then wrap it in plastic. Set aside in a warm, draught free place for 1 hour or until doubled in size.
4. To push back the dough, use your fist. Make 16 balls by dividing the mixture into parts of about 30g each. Add a little additional olive oil to the balls and gently flip to coat. Air fryer basket should be lightly greased. Put half the balls into the air fryer basket and space them out. Cook at 190C for 10 minutes, or until golden brown. To a wire rack, transfer the balls. Remaining balls should be cooked. 5 Horizontally split the broccoli. Ricotta is spread over the foundation, then prosciutto is added on top. To serve, top with the head of the broccoli.

Air fryer saltimbocca

Prep time : 5mins
Cook time: 12 mins
Serve 2

Ingredients

- 2 small chicken breast fillets
- 4 fresh sage leaves
- 4 slices prosciutto
- 1 bunch thick asparagus spears
- Extra virgin olive oil, to drizzle
- Lemon wedges, to serve
- Bought hollandaise sauce, to serve

Preparation Instructions :

1. Add two sage leaves to the top of each piece of chicken, then wrap with prosciutto slices to hold the leaves in place. Put the bundles in the air fryer with the seam facing up. Use oil to mist. 8 minutes of cooking at 180 °C.
2. Spray some oil on the air fryer before adding the asparagus. Cook chicken for 4 minutes, or until fully done.
3. On serving dishes, arrange the chicken and asparagus. Serve with lemon wedges and sauce and drizzle with oil.

Air fryer Pork crackling

Prep time : 5mins
Cook time: 30 mins
Serve 4-6

Ingredients

- 1kg piece boneless pork belly, rind scored
- 2 tsp sea salt flakes
- Olive oil spray

Preparation Instructions :

1. For three minutes, heat the air fryer to 200°C. With a paper towel, pat the meat dry. Pork rind should be salted.

2. Spray the air fryer basket with oil and add the meat. Timer should be set for 25 minutes, or until the rind begins to crackle. Set the thermostat to 160°C. Set a 30-minute timer and cook the pork until it is soft and done. Serve and enjoy.

3. On serving dishes, arrange the chicken and asparagus. Serve with lemon wedges and sauce and drizzle with oil.

Air fryer sticky pork belly bites

Prep time : 15mins
Cook time: 40 mins
Serve 4-6

Ingredients

- 1kg piece boneless pork belly
- 3 tsp smoked paprika
- 1 tsp onion powder
- Olive oil spray
- 50g butter
- 2 tbsp barbecue sauce
- 2 tsp sriracha

- 1 tbsp brown sugar
- 2 tsp plain flour
- 1/2 tsp garlic powder
- Sticky golden syrup sauce
- 2 tbsp golden syrup
- 1 tbsp bourbon

Preparation Instructions :

1. Make 4 cm-long chunks of pork belly. Put in a small dish.

2. Sugar, paprika, flour, onion, and garlic powder are all combined in a bowl. Toss to coat the meat after evenly spreading. 2 hours in the refrigerator (do not cover the pork with plastic wrap as it needs to dry out).

3. Set the air fryer to 200 °C. Spray plenty of oil on the meat. properly season. Put the air fryer basket in the basket with the meat. Cook for 15 to 20 minutes, shaking basket halfway through, or until meat is just starting to brown and is well cooked. Toss into a bowl. Repeat with the remaining pork.

4. Make the sticky golden syrup sauce in the meanwhile. In a small saucepan over medium heat, combine the butter, golden syrup, barbecue sauce, bourbon, and sriracha. Season. Cook for 2 to 3 minutes while stirring, or until mixture is smooth and melted. Simmer for a while. The sauce should thicken after 3 to 4 minutes of simmering. Get rid of the heat.

5. To serve, drizzle the sauce over the meat.

Air fryer turkey crown

Prep time : 5mins
Cook time: 50 mins
Serve 6

Ingredients

- 1.7kg turkey crown
- 1 tsp vegetable oil
- 1 tsp dried mixed herbs
- 1 clementine, halved
- 1 shallot, halved
- 2 garlic cloves, bashed
- a few fresh herb sprigs, such as sage, thyme or oregano

Preparation Instructions :

1. Use the air fryer's preheat feature to warm it or set it to 180C for two minutes. Apply kitchen paper to the turkey crown to help it dry, then massage the oil all over it. After properly seasoning, sprinkle the skin with the dry herbs. Place the clementine halves, shallot, garlic cloves, and fresh herb sprigs into the cavity, if the crown permits. If this isn't possible, tuck them around the crown in the air-fryer basket. In any case, make sure the skin-side-down position of the turkey crown in the air fryer basket.
2. Cook for 30 minutes, then flip the crown over and cook for a further 20 to 30 minutes, or until the juices flow clear when a knife is inserted in the thickest portion or a meat thermometer is inserted and reads 145°F.

Air fryer chicken thighs

Prep time : 2 mins
Cook time: 25 mins
Serve 4

Ingredients

- 1 tsp paprika
- ½ tsp mixed herbs
- ½ tsp garlic granules (optional)
- 4 chicken thighs, bone in
- 1 tsp olive oil

Preparation Instructions :

1. In a bowl, mix the paprika, herbs, and, if using, garlic granules with 12 tsp. salt and 12 tsp. freshly ground black pepper. Onto a dish, scatter. After applying the oil and spice mixture to the chicken thighs, coat them.
2. Cook for 10 minutes at 180C with the skin-side down in the air fryer basket. Once cooked through and the skin is crispy, flip the meat over and cook for a further 10-15 minutes. Use a knife to puncture the thickest portion of the thigh to examine whether the fluids flow clear to determine whether they are done. To prevent the skin from softening, remove from the Ninja foodi air fryer right away.

Chicken, bacon and creamed corn roll-ups

Prep time : 15 mins
Cook time: 20 mins
Serve 2

Ingredients

- 1 chicken breast fillet
- 90g can creamed corn
- 60g cream cheese, chopped, at room temperature
- 40g pre-grated 3 cheese blend
- 1 tbsp chopped fresh coriander
- 4 streaky bacon rashers
- Tomato salsa, to serve

Preparation Instructions :

1. Slice the chicken breast in half horizontally using a long, sharp knife. The chicken breasts should be pounded with a meat mallet to a thickness of around 5mm.
2. In a bowl, mix the corn, cream cheese, cheese blend, and coriander. One chicken piece should have half the mixture on top. Add the remaining mixture on top of the last piece of chicken. Roll the chicken carefully from the short end in order to enclose. Each chicken piece is encased in two slices of bacon. With toothpicks, secure.
3. Spray oil on the air fryer's basket. When the chicken is fully cooked, place it in the air fryer basket and cook it at 180°C for 15 minutes, rotating the chicken once halfway through.
4. Discard toothpicks. Slice the chicken and serve with salsa .

BBQ Baby Back Ribs

Prep time : 5 mins
Cook time: 35mins
Serve 4

Ingredients

- 1360 g baby back pork ribs
- 1 tablespoon white sugar
- 1 teaspoon smoked paprika
- ½ teaspoon ground black pepper
- ½ teaspoon granulated onion
- 41.67 ml barbeque sauce
- 1 tablespoon brown sugar
- 1 teaspoon sweet paprika
- 1 teaspoon granulated garlic
- ½ teaspoon ground cumin
- ¼ teaspoon Greek seasoning (Optional)

Preparation Instructions :

1. Set the Ninja foodi air fryer to 350 degrees Fahrenheit (175 degrees C).
2. Remove the ribs' back membrane. Cut the ribs into four equal pieces.
3. In a separate bowl, mix together the brown sugar, white sugar, smoked paprika, granulated garlic, pepper, cumin, onion, and Greek seasoning. Rub ribs with spice mixture all over. In the air fryer basket, put the ribs.
4. Ribs should be cooked in the air fryer that has been warmed for 30 minutes, flipping once. Apply barbecue sauce and continue to air-fry for 5 more minutes.

Steak and Mushrooms

Prep time : 5 mins
Cook time: 10 mins
Serve 4

Ingredients

- 450 g beef sirloin steak, cut into 1-inch cubes
- 226 g button mushrooms, sliced
- 32 ml Worcestershire sauce
- 1 tablespoon olive oil
- 1 teaspoon parsley flakes
- 1 teaspoon paprika
- 1 teaspoon crushed chile flakes

Preparation Instructions :

1. In a bowl, combine the steak, mushrooms, parsley, paprika, olive oil, and chili flakes. For at least 4 hours or overnight, cover and chill. Take out of the fridge 30 minutes before cooking.
2. Set a 400°F air fryer temperature (200 degrees C).
3. The beef mixture's marinade should be drained and discarded. Put the steak and the mushrooms in the air fryer's basket.
4. Cook for five minutes in the preheated air fryer. Cook for five more minutes after tossing. Place the steak and the mushrooms on a serving platter and give them five minutes to rest.

Air Fryer Steak and Cheese Melts

Prep time : 10 mins
Cook time: 25 mins
Serve 4

Ingredients

- 453 g beef rib-eye steak, thinly sliced
- 2 tablespoons Worcestershire sauce

- 1 tablespoon reduced-sodium soy sauce
- 113 g sliced baby portobello mushrooms
- 1 tablespoon olive oil
- ½ teaspoon ground mustard
- 4 hoagie rolls

- 1 medium onion, sliced into petals
- ½ green bell pepper, thinly sliced
- ½ teaspoon salt
- ¼ teaspoon ground black pepper
- 4 slices Provolone cheese

Preparation Instructions :

1. Add Worcestershire and soy sauce to the meat in a bowl. For four to eight hours, cover and chill. After taking it out of the fridge, let it sit at room temperature for 30 minutes.
2. The Ninja foodi air fryer should be preheated to 380 degrees F. (190 degrees C).
3. In a large bowl, mix the onion, mushrooms, and bell pepper. Stir in the ground mustard, olive oil, salt, and pepper.
4. Hoagie rolls should be cooked for around two minutes in the air fryer's basket until toasted. Put rolls on a platter.
5. Steak should be cooked for three minutes in the air fryer basket. Cook for another minute while stirring. Place on a platter.
6. Place a vegetable mixture in the air fryer's basket and cook for five minutes. For about 5 more minutes, stir and simmer until softened.
7. Add steak to the vegetable mixture by stirring. Overlap the cheese slices as you place them. Cook for about 3 minutes, or until cheese is melted and bubbling. Serve the mixture right away by spooning it onto the bread.

Steak Bites with Soy Sauce

Prep time : 5 mins
Cook time: 6 mins
Serve 3

Ingredients

- 253 g beef rib-eye steaks
- 85 ml oyster sauce
- 2 tablespoons reduced-sodium soy sauce
- 2 tablespoons sweet soy sauce
- 1 tablespoon sesame oil
- 1 tablespoon brown sugar
- ½ teaspoon toasted sesame seeds

Preparation Instructions :

1. Cut meat into bite-size pieces. Place steak pieces into a resealable plastic bag.
2. Oyster sauce, soy sauce, sweet soy sauce, sesame oil, and brown sugar should all be combined in one bowl. Mix the mixture before pouring it over the steak pieces to marinate them. Marinate for 30 minutes.

3. Set to 400°F air fryer temperature (200 degrees C).

4. Wrap a round of perforated parchment paper around the air fryer basket. The steak should be drained of the marinade before being placed on the paper.

5. Shake the basket after 3 minutes to ensure that the steak bits are cooked to your preferred doneness. Air-frying takes about 6 minutes.

6. Before serving, take the steak bits out of the ninja foodi air fryer and top with toasted sesame seeds.

Steak Tips and Portobello Mushrooms

Prep time : 5 mins
Cook time: 10 mins
Serve 3

Ingredients

- 85 ml olive oil
- 1 tablespoon coconut aminos (soy-free seasoning sauce)
- 2 teaspoons Montreal steak seasoning
- ½ teaspoon garlic powder
- 2 strip steaks, cut into 3/4-inch pieces
- 113 g portobello mushrooms, quartered

Preparation Instructions :

1. In a small bowl, mix the olive oil, coconut aminos, steak seasoning, and garlic powder. Add the steak pieces, stir thoroughly, and marinate for 15 minutes.

2. Heat the air fryer to 390 degrees Fahrenheit (200 degrees C). With parchment paper that has been perforated, line the bottom of the air fryer basket.

3. Drain the marinade off the steak pieces. Place a steak and portobello mushroom quarters in the ninja foodi air fryer basket.

4. Cook for five minutes in the preheated air fryer. Take the basket out, stir the meat and mushrooms, and cook for a further 4 minutes.

Air Fryer Chicken Cordon Bleu

Prep time : 15 mins
Cook time: 20 mins
Serve 2

Ingredients

- 2 boneless, skinless chicken breasts
- 1 tablespoon Dijon mustard
- salt and ground black pepper to taste
- 4 slices deli Swiss cheese

- 4 slices deli ham
- 32 g all-purpose flour
- 250 g panko bread crumbs
- cooking spray
- 2 toothpicks
- 1 egg, beaten
- 41.67 g grated Parmesan cheese

Preparation Instructions :

1. On a flat work surface, place a chicken breast. Be cautious not to cut all the way through to the opposite side when you slice horizontally across the centre. Spread the two sides apart like an open book. Place the chicken breast between two heavy plastic sheets on a stable, level surface. Lightly pound the chicken breast with a meat mallet's smooth side to a thickness of 1/4 inch. Repeat with the last chicken breast.
2. Sprinkle salt and pepper on each chicken breast. Dijon mustard should be applied. On each breast, place a piece of cheese. Each should have 2 slices of ham and 1 piece of cheese on top. With a toothpick, roll each breast up and fasten.
3. You should put flour in a small bowl. Put the egg in a different bowl. In a third bowl, combine panko bread crumbs and grated Parmesan.
4. Set a 350°F air fryer temperature (175 degrees C).
5. Chicken breasts should be dredged in flour in the meantime. Dip into beaten egg, letting any extra drain back into the dish as you do so. Place breaded chicken breasts on a platter and spray with nonstick spray after pressing into the bread crumb mixture to cover both sides. Place breaded chicken in the air fryer basket in a single layer after letting stand for 5 minutes while the air fryer warms up.
6. After 10 minutes in the preheated air fryer, turn the chicken breasts over and coat any dry areas with nonstick spray. Cook for another 8 minutes or until the middle of the chicken is no longer pink. In the middle, an instant-read thermometer should indicate at least 165 degrees Fahrenheit (74 degrees C).

Rosemary garlic Lamb chops

Prep time : 10 mins
Cook time: 14 mins
Serve 4

Ingredients

- 567 g rack of lamb , about 7-8 chops
- 30 ml chopped fresh rosemary
- 5 ml garlic powder or 3 cloves garlic, minced
- 45 ml olive oil
- 5 ml salt , or to taste
- 2.5 ml black pepper , or to taste

Preparation Instructions :

1. The lamb rack should be dried using paper towels. If necessary, take the silver skin from the back of the ribs. Separate the chops into pieces.
2. Olive oil, rosemary, garlic, salt, and pepper should all be combined in a big bowl. Gently stir the lamb into the marinade after adding it. For up to overnight, cover and marinate the food.
3. The Ninja foodi Air Fryer should be preheated for 4 minutes at 380°F/195°C. Lamb chops should be placed in a single layer, not overlapping, in an oil-sprayed air fryer basket.
4. Turn over and continue air-frying for an additional 3-6 minutes, or until the food is cooked to your preference, at 380°F/195°C. Serve hot.

Braised lamb shanks

Prep time : 15 mins
Cook time: 14 2 hours and 20 mins
Serve 4

Ingredients

- 4 lamb shanks
- ½ teaspoon freshly ground black pepper
- 2 tablespoons olive oil
- 700 ml beef broth, divided

- 1½ teaspoons kosher salt
- 4 garlic cloves, crushed
- 4 to 6 sprigs fresh rosemary
- 2 tablespoons balsamic vinegar

Preparation Instructions :

1 . Place the lamb shanks on the baking/drip pan after seasoning with salt and pepper. Rub the lamb all over with the minced garlic. Apply olive oil to the seasoned lamb shanks and cover with rosemary before cooking.
2 . Place the lamb-filled prepared pan in rack Position. Set the temperature first to Roast for 20 minutes at 425°F and then to Low for 2 hours at 250°F.
3 . While cooking, the lamb was turned once. When the aif fryer is set to Low, add 2 cups of the broth and vinegar. One hour of simmering time remains; add the remaining broth.
4 . When the lamb easily pulls from the bone, it is cooked.

Air Fryer garlic butter salmon

Prep time : 5 mins
Cook time: 10 mins
Serve 2

Ingredients

- 2 (170 g) boneless, skin-on salmon fillets (preferably wild-caught)
- 2 tablespoons butter, melted
- 1 teaspoon garlic, minced
- 1 teaspoon fresh Italian parsley, chopped (or 1/4 teaspoon dried)
- salt and pepper to taste

Preparation Instructions :

1. Set the air fryer to 360 degrees of heat.
2. Salt and pepper the fresh salmon before adding the melted butter, garlic, and parsley to a bowl.
3. Place the salmon fillets, skin side down, side by side in the air fryer after brushing them with the garlic butter mixture.
4. Salmon should be cooked for about 10 minutes or until it flakes easily with a knife or fork. Serve and enjoy.

Air Fryer tuna steak

Prep time : 20 mins
Cook time: 4 mins
Serve 2

Ingredients

- 2 (170g) boneless and skinless yellowfin tuna steaks
- 2 teaspoons honey
- 1 teaspoon sesame oil
- green onions, sliced optional
- 85 g soy sauce
- 1 teaspoon grated ginger
- 1/2 teaspoon rice vinegar
- sesame seeds optional

Preparation Instructions :

1. Take the tuna steaks out of the refrigerator.
2. Soy sauce, honey, ginger that has been grated, sesame oil, and rice vinegar should all be combined in a big bowl.

3. Tuna steaks should be marinated for 20 to 30 minutes covered in the fridge.
4. Tuna steaks should be cooked for 4 minutes in an air fryer that has been preheated to 380 degrees.
5. Sliced air-fried tuna steaks can be enjoyed right away after resting for a few minutes. If desired, garnish with sesame seeds or green onions.

Air fryer bang bang Shrimp

Prep time : 10 mins
Cook time: 20 mins
Serve 3-4

Ingredients

- ¾ cup mayonnaise
- ⅓ cup sweet chili sauce
- 1-3 teaspoons sriracha, or to taste
- 1 ½ pounds large shrimp, peeled and deveined, tail on
- ⅔ cup cornstarch
- ½ cup buttermilk
- 2 cups panko bread crumbs
- ½ teaspoon kosher salt

Preparation Instructions :

1. Mayonnaise, sweet chili sauce, and sriracha should all be properly combined in a small mixing dish. In a small dish or a plastic zipper bag, put the cornstarch. Put the buttermilk in a different, small bowl. Salt and bread crumbs should be combined in a third small bowl.
2. Your air fryer should be preheated to 400 degrees F.
3. The shrimp should be thoroughly dried before being placed in the cornstarch bag (or dish). To thoroughly coat the shrimp, seal the bag and shake it. Put the shrimp on a platter after shaking off any extra cornstarch.
4. Working in batches, coat the shrimp with buttermilk before coating them with breadcrumbs and pushing them down hard to ensure the crumbs stick. Place the coated shrimp in the air fryer in a single layer with some distance between them (you may need to work in batches). Lightly mist them with cooking spray.
5. To properly cook the shrimp, air fried them for a further 5 minutes, turn them over, and then spritz them with cooking oil.
6. Repeat with the remaining shrimp that have been coated before transferring the cooked shrimp to a medium mixing bowl.
7. When all of the shrimp are cooked, drizzle the bang bang sauce over them and give them a quick toss to coat.
8. Serve immediately after adding a parsley garnish.

Air Fryer Blackened Shrimp

Prep time : 5 mins

Cook time: 6 mins
Serve 4

Ingredients

- 453 g large shrimp , peeled and deveined
- 1 tablespoon blackened seasoning
- Lemon Wedges
- 2 tablespoons olive oil
- Favorite Dipping Sauce
- Parsley , chopped

Preparation Instructions :

1. For five minutes, preheat the ninja foodi air fryer to 400 degrees. Olive oil should be mixed with shrimp in a mixing basin, with any extra oil being drained off the bottom.
2. Sprinkle blackened seasoning on shrimp. Grease the air fryer basket gently when it's hot. Put shrimp in.
3. Cook for 5–6 minutes at 400 degrees, shaking the pan once halfway through. Cook until shrimp are pink, curled, and cooked through.
4. With your favorite dipping sauces, remove and serve. Parsley and lemon wedges are optional.

Air Fryer Honey sriracha salmon

Prep time : 3 mins
Cook time: 7 mins
Serve 2

Ingredients

- 680 g salmon
- 2 tbsp sriracha
- cooking spray
- 3 tbsp honey
- salt to taste

Preparation Instructions :

1. Combine the honey and sriracha sauce in a small bowl. Mix thoroughly.
2. After salting the salmon, cover it with the honey mixture. Allow it to rest for 20 minutes at room temperature.
3. Place the salmon in the air fryer, and cook it for 7 minutes at 400 degrees. Enjoy!

Air Fryer Cajun Scallops

Prep time : 5 mins
Cook time: 6 mins
Serve 2

Ingredients

- 4-6 Sea scallops
- Cooking spray

- Kosher salt to taste
- Cajun seasoning

Preparation Instructions :

1. Set your air fryer's temperature to 400 F.
2. Out of the refrigerator, quickly rinse your fresh sea scallops in cold water. Use your fingers to pull out the side muscle, then use paper towels to dry it off.
3. The basket should be lined with aluminum foil and gently sprayed with cooking spray after your air fryer has been prepared. Cooking oil should be drizzled on the scallops lightly. Kosher salt and cajun spice should then be sprinkled all over the fish.
4. All the scallops should be cooked for three minutes in the air fryer. Cook for a further 3 minutes on the other side, or until they are opaque and internal temperature reaches at least 130 F.
5. Serve alongside roasted veggies or with pasta, salad, or both.

Air Fryer crab stuffed mushrooms

Prep time : 15 mins
Cook time: 18 mins
Serve 4

Ingredients

- 900 g Baby Bella Mushrooms
- 2 teaspoons Salt Blend
- 2 Celery Ribs, diced
- 128 g Seasoned Bread Crumbs, like Progresso Seasoned
- 1 large egg
- 32 g Parmesan Cheese, shredded, divided
- 1 teaspoon Oregano
- Cooking Spray, Olive Oil spray preferred
- ¼ Red Onion, diced
- 8 ounces Lump Crab
- 1 teaspoon Hot Sauce

Preparation Instructions :

1. Set the oven or air fryer to 400°F.
2. Cooking spray should be used on a baking sheet or Air Fryer tray. Mushroom stems should be bent. Place the mushrooms top down and coat with cooking spray made with olive oil. All of the mushrooms should be seasoned with salt. Set aside.
3. onion and celery into dice. Combine the egg, breadcrumbs, crab, onions, celery, oregano, and spicy sauce.
4. Each mushroom should be filled inside, then the filling should be piled up a bit to form a small mound.
5. Top with the remaining Parmesan flakes.
6. In the ninja foodi Air Fryer, bake for around 8 to 9 minutes. Bake in the oven for 16 to 18 minutes.

Air Fryer bacon wrapped shrimp

Prep time : 15 mins
Cook time: 10 mins
Serve 3-4

Ingredients

- 453 g bacon, thinly sliced
- 113.4g maple syrup
- 1 teaspoon garlic powder
- Salt and pepper to taste
- 453 g raw jumbo shrimp, peeled and deveined
- 4 tablespoons low sodium soy sauce
- ¼ teaspoon red pepper flakes
- Optional: garnish with green onion

Preparation Instructions :

1. Make a lengthwise cut through each piece of bacon. Start at the tail of the shrimp, overlap the first piece of bacon to help keep it on, and then wrap up and around the shrimp with as little overlap as possible until you reach the top of the shrimp. On a baking sheet, place the shrimp that have been wrapped.
2. Salt, pepper, red pepper flakes, garlic powder, maple syrup, soy sauce, and other seasonings should all be combined in a small bowl. Garnish the shrimp with the glaze using a basting brush. Then coat the other side after flipping the shrimp.
3. 3. 400°F should be the air fryer's set temperature. Leaving room around them, add the shrimp to the air fryer. Flip them after 4 minutes of cooking. After frying them for an additional 6 minutes or until the bacon is crispy, brush them with extra sauce. Serve hot and enjoy.

Air Fryer catfish

Prep time : 40 mins
Cook time: 20 mins
Serve 3-4

Ingredients

- 2 catfish fillets
- ½ tablespoon olive oil
- 1 ½ tablespoons blackening seasoning (or Cajun seasoning)
- ½ teaspoon dried oregano
- ½ teaspoon black pepper
- ¼ teaspoon cayenne pepper
- Fresh chopped parsley, for garnish
- 128 g milk (or buttermilk)
- ½ teaspoon kosher salt
- ½ teaspoon garlic powder
- Lemon wedges, for serving

Preparation Instructions :

1. Pour the milk (or buttermilk) over the catfish fillets and let them soak for at least 30 minutes

before cooking. This will help the fishy flavor to be neutralized.

2. Blackening or Cajun seasoning, oregano, salt, pepper, garlic powder, and cayenne pepper should all be combined in a small bowl before being set aside.

3. Pre-heat your ninja foodi air fryer to 400 degrees when you're ready to cook. Take the fish out, then pat it dry. Olive oil should be applied to the fillets. Each fillet should be fully covered by the spice mixture after being sprinkled on both sides. Put the fillets within in a single layer. Spray the fish's heads.

4. 10 minutes of air frying at 400 degrees F. Fry the fish for a further 10 to 12 minutes (20 to 22 minutes total), or until it is cooked to your taste. Lemon wedges and parsley are served alongside.

Air Fryer Oysters

Prep time : 10 mins
Cook time: 10 mins
Serve 2

Ingredients

- 450 g raw, shucked oysters
- 1 teaspoon cajun seasoning
- ¼ teaspoon black pepper
- 1 tablespoon milk
- Lemon wedges, for serving

- 64 g all-purpose flour
- ½ teaspoon kosher salt
- 1 large egg
- 192 g breadcrumbs
- Melted garlic butter, for serving

Preparation Instructions :

1. Set your air fryer to 350 degrees Fahrenheit.

2. The oysters should be shucked, cleaned, and let to drain in a colander. With paper towels, pat the shucked oysters dry.

3. Mix the flour, cajun spice, salt, and pepper in a small basin. Whisk the egg and milk in a separate dish. Panko breadcrumbs should be put in a third bowl.

4. The oysters should be dredged in the flour mixture, then dipped in the egg mixture before being rolled in bread crumbs to coat. Put the oysters in the basket in a single layer and give them a gentle cooking spraying.

5. Cook for four minutes in the Ninja foodi air fryer. The oysters are cooked for a further 4 minutes after being flipped, after which they are gently sprayed with cooking oil. Serve.

Air Fryer Cheesy Tuna Flautas

Prep time : 15 mins
Cook time: 5 mins
Serve 4

Ingredients

- 8 small flour tortillas
- 1/8 tsp salt
- 1/8 tsp ancho chile powder
- 1/2 cup cheddar cheese, shredded
- 64 g sour cream for dipping, optional
- 1 can Wild Selections tuna
- 1/8 tsp garlic powder
- 1/2 tsp cilantro, chopped
- 1/2 cup guacamole for dipping, optional

Preparation Instructions :

1. Tuna, salt, garlic powder, ancho chile powder, and cilantro should all be combined in a bowl.
2. Each tortilla should have some cheddar cheese sprinkled on top of it.
3. On top of the cheese, spread roughly a TBSP of the tuna mixture. If desired, add extra cheese on top!
4. Each tortilla should be rolled and toothpick-secured. Place everything in the Air Fryer's bottom in a single layer and secure.
5. Cook for 5-7 minutes at 350 degrees, checking after the fourth minute. Remove from the Air Fryer when golden and crispy, and allow to cool for a while.
6. Serve with sour cream and guacamole!

Air Fryer Salmon Patties

Prep time : 10 mins
Cook time: 10 mins
Serve 4

Ingredients

- 1 small salmon fillet, skin removed (about 140 g)
- 1 large egg
- 1 tablespoon chopped fresh chives
- 1/2 teaspoon garlic powder
- 1/8 teaspoon ground black pepper
- 85 g almond flour
- 1/2 medium-sized onion, chopped
- 1 tablespoon freshly squeezed lemon juice
- 1/2 teaspoon kosher salt

Preparation Instructions :

1. Add all the ingredients to a food processor along with the salmon fillet that has been cut into small pieces.
2. On high speed, blend everything until just a few tiny bits of salmon, onion, and chives are visible. Four 3-inch-diameter patties should be formed; place in the refrigerator for 30 minutes.
3. Apply nonstick cooking spray to the air fryer basket. Spray cooking spray on top of each patty before placing it in a single layer in the bottom of the basket.
4. For 10 to 12 minutes at 400°F, or until well cooked and crisp on the exterior, air fried the food.

Crispy Air Fryer Tempeh

Prep time : 15 mins

Cook time: 15 mins

Serve 4

Ingredients

- 11 (225 g) package tempeh sliced into 1/2"-1" cubes
- 1 tablespoon avocado oil or neutral oil of choice
- 1 tablespoon coconut aminos or soy sauce
- 1 teaspoon toasted sesame oil
- 1 teaspoon garlic powder
- 1/2 teaspoon sea salt or pink salt or salt to suit personal preference

Preparation Instructions :

1. Set the air fryer to 390 °F.
2. Slice the tempeh into 1" to 2" cubes and put the cubes into a large mixing dish.
3. In the same bowl, combine the salt, garlic powder, sesame oil, avocado oil, and coconut aminos. Toss to combine. Set aside for 10 minutes to marinate.
4. After the tempeh has completed marinating, arrange it in a single layer in the air fryer basket or tray and cook it there for 15 minutes, or until it is firm, crispy, and golden. Enjoy!

Smoky Tempeh Sandwich

Prep time : 40 mins

Cook time: 15 mins

Serve 2

Ingredients

- 2 tablespoons soy sauce
- 1 tablespoon ketchup
- 1/2 teaspoon paprika
- 225 g block of tempeh
- 4 tomato slices
- 1 avocado
- 1 tablespoon rice vinegar
- 1/2 teaspoon garlic powder
- 1/2 teaspoon liquid smoke
- 4 slices of whole grain bread
- 4 lettuce leaves

Preparation Instructions :

1. In a large bowl or dish for marinating, combine the soy sauce, rice vinegar, ketchup, garlic

powder, paprika, and liquid smoke. Set aside.

2. Strip the tempeh after thinly slicing. Place in marinade, and the longer the better, let marinate for at least 30 minutes. Keep any marinade that is left over.

3. After the tempeh has marinated, air fried it for 10 to 15 minutes at 325°F, watching it carefully to prevent scorching. The baking process will require more time—probably 10-15 minutes on each side.

4. To add more flavor, you may cover the strips of tempeh in any remaining marinade.

5. If desired, toast pieces of bread. Half an avocado should be used to assemble each sandwich after being sliced or mashed.

6. Top with lettuce, tomatoes, and slices of tempeh. When desired, add more condiments. Place a slice of bread on top. Enjoy!

Tofu with Honey Garlic Sauce

Prep time : 10 mins

Cook time: 18 mins

Serve 2-4

Ingredients

- 390 g extra firm tofu
- 1 tsp Garlic Powder
- 1/2 tsp Onion Powder
- Cooking Spray
- 96 ml Chicken Broth
- 2 tbsp Soy sauce
- 1/2 tsp Ground Ginger
- 1 Tbsp Water

- 1 tbsp Corn Starch
- 1/2 tsp Paprika
- 1/2 tsp Salt
- Honey Garlic Sauce
- 43 ml Honey Can add more if you like it sweeter!
- 2 tsp Garlic minced
- 1/2 Tbsp Cornstarch

Preparation Instructions :

1. To remove extra moisture, place the tofu in the middle of a dry, thin dishtowel and gently press. Tofu should be cut into 1 x 1 inch pieces.

2. Put the pieces in a large bowl or zip-top bag. Add the salt, paprika, onion powder, garlic powder, and cornstarch. Shake or shut the bag and toss it around until the tofu is well covered.

3. Spray the ninja foodi air fryer basket, then add the cubes in a single layer. Cooking spray the tofu's tops (optional; use parchment paper for the air fryer for simple cleanup).

4. 18 minutes at 360F in the air fryer. Shake the basket once the ten minutes are up. Reposition the tofu over the basket in a single layer, and cook for an additional 8 minutes at 360F.

5. In a saucepan over medium heat, add chicken stock, honey, soy sauce, garlic, and ginger; bring to a slow boil while the tofu is cooking. Reduce heat, cover, and simmer sauce for about 5 minutes, stirring often to blend flavors.

6. In a small bowl, stir together the water and cornstarch. Pour into the pan and cook for five minutes to thicken the sauce. Once the tofu has finished cooking.

7. Place in a bowl and stir with 1/2 cup honey garlic sauce.

8. When serving the tofu, add more sauce as desired. Enjoy!

Crispy Breaded tofu

Prep time : 18 mins
Cook time: 12 mins
Serve 4

Ingredients

- 340 g extra-firm tofu
- ¾ teaspoon garlic powder
- 85 g panko breadcrumbs (more if needed, see note 1)
- Oil spray (olive oil or grapeseed oil)
- Salt (optional)

- 2 tablespoons tamari (or soy sauce)
- 2 tablespoons cornstarch
- Black pepper (ideally coarsely ground)

Preparation Instructions :

1. Cut the tofu into 34-inch (2.2 cm) pieces. With a fresh kitchen towel, pat dry.

2. Place the cubes in a small bowl. Sprinkle garlic powder on top of the tofu after adding tamari. Toss the coat lightly with your hands. Turning the cubes every few minutes, let marinate for 6 to 8 minutes or until most, but not all, of the tamari is absorbed.

3. Sprinkle cornstarch on top of the tofu to add more. Toss the coat lightly with your hands. (There shouldn't be any visible dry cornstarch; if you do, keep tossing.)

4. One cube at a time, wet the cube by spinning it in the remaining tamari in the bottom of the dish with one hand. Using panko, coat the tofu in all directions (use your other dry hand to press the panko into tofu). Repeat with more breaded tofu in an air frying basket. (Lay out the cubes in the basket in a single layer.)

5. Give the tofu a generous oiling. There is no need to preheat the air fryer before baking for 10 minutes at 400°F (200°C). Shake the basket and bake for a further 1 to 3 minutes, or until crispy and golden brown. Optional, but helps with browning.

6. If necessary, add extra salt to the tofu along with black pepper. While still hot from the oven, Serve.

Air Fryer Bang Bang Tofu

Prep time : 5 mins
Cook time: 8 mins
Serve 4

Ingredients

- 1 (390 g) package extra-firm tofu

- 2 tablespoons toasted sesame oil

- 128 g mayonnaise
- 1 ½ tablespoons Sriracha sauce
- 1 green onion, chopped
- 64 ml sweet chili sauce
- 192 g panko bread crumbs

Preparation Instructions :

1. On a platter covered with a lot of paper towels, put the tofu. Add another dish on top and extra paper towels. Press the tofu for 30 minutes with a 3- to 5-pound weight placed on top. Tofu should be cut into 1/2-inch cubes and any liquid should be drained and removed.
2. Cubed tofu should be placed in a dish with sesame oil on top. Stir gently, then set aside for 20 minutes.
3. Make bang bang sauce in the meantime by blending mayonnaise, sweet chili sauce, and Sriracha sauce. Put panko in a different bowl.
4. Set the air fryer to 400 degrees Fahrenheit (200 degrees C).
5. Tofu and bang bang sauce should be mixed well. Tofu should not overlap as it is placed in the air fryer basket after being coated in panko bread crumbs. You might have to do this in batches depending on the size of your air fryer.
6. For five minutes, cook. Cook for three more minutes while shaking. Serve with the leftover bang bang sauce and green onion garnish.

Air Fryer Karaagi Tofu

Prep time : 20 mins
Cook time: 15 mins
Serve 2

Ingredients

- 1 (390 g) block firm tofu, twice frozen
- 1 clove of garlic, grated
- 2 tablespoons soy sauce
- 1 teaspoon sake
- 2 tablespoons all purpose flour
- 2 teaspoons ginger, grated
- 1 tablepsoon water or vegetable broth
- 1 tablespoon mirin
- 1 teaspoon sesame oil
- 2 tablespoons potato starch

Preparation Instructions :

1. Simply put the tofu in the freezer (in the packaging is acceptable) to double-freeze it. After being frozen, place for a day in the refrigerator to defrost, then overnight return to the freezer. One frozen, place in refrigerator to defrost once more. Before using, make sure the tofu is fully defrosted. Tofu should be cut or split into big pieces.
2. Ginger, garlic, water/broth, soy sauce, sake, and mirin should all be combined. Put in a large dish.
3. To thoroughly coat the tofu, add it to the marinade and thoroughly stir. Drizzle the sesame oil over the top and quickly toss. Give the food 10 minutes to marinate. Most if not all of the

sauce should get soaked up.

4. Toss the tofu with the flour to coat. After the tofu has been properly covered with flour, dust potato starch over it and give it one more thorough toss.

5. Put each piece of tofu into the air fryer. Be sure the tofu pieces are not touching and are not touching one another. After five minutes of air frying at 350°F, gently mist the pieces with oil. Continue air frying for a further 10 minutes, or until it is crispy and golden.

6. If preferred, garnish the karaage with a few salt flakes and lemon slices.

Air Fryer sweet and smoky tempeh

Prep time : 5 mins
Cook time: 10 mins
Serve 2

Ingredients

- 225 g tempeh (1 package)
- 1 ½ tablespoon maple syrup
- 2 teaspoons cooking oil such as avocado or grapeseed - For oil-free, omit or sub 1 Tbsp tahini.
- 2 teaspoons sriracha
- ½ teaspoon liquid smoke
- scant ½ teaspoon fine sea salt
- ¼ teaspoon black pepper

- 1 ½ tablespoons tamari or soy sauce

- 1 teaspoon apple cider vinegar
- ½ teaspoon garlic powder
- ¼ teaspoon smoked paprika

Preparation Instructions :

1. To prepare the marinade, combine all of the ingredients in a big bowl or dish, excluding the tempeh. The tempeh should be cut into 24 or 36 squares. I like smaller pieces because they give the tasty marinade greater surface area. There will be about. 12 to 34 inch.

2. Make sure all of the tempeh is thoroughly covered with the marinade before tossing it in. Set a 30-minute timer. Pour the marinade from the bottom of the bowl over the tempeh one or twice during that time.

3. After the tempeh has been marinated, place the rack in the air fryer basket after adding 3/4 to 1 cup of water to the bottom. Set the air fryer's temperature to 350 degrees. Place the tempeh in a single layer once it has been heated. It should be sitting above the water line.

4. Cook for around 10 minutes, monitoring to make sure it isn't burning during the midway and final minutes. When the tempeh is scorching hot and the edges have caramelized, it is ready. Serve warm.

Tempeh Bacon

Prep time : 20 mins
Cook time: 15 mins

Serving : 14-16 pieces

Ingredients

- 225 g tempeh
- 3 tablespoons light soy sauce
- 2 teaspoon date syrup
- 1 ½ teaspoon liquid smoke
- ½ teaspoon granulated garlic

- Tempeh Marinade
- 3 teaspoons maple syrup
- 2 teaspoons apple cider vinegar
- ½ teaspoon smoked paprika
- ½ teaspoon onion powder

Preparation Instructions :

1. To make the tempeh less bitter, steam it. In a small or medium saucepan (or steamer) with 3/4 inch of water, place the tempeh log. For about 10 minutes, steam over medium-low heat with the pot's cover on.
2. The marinade ingredients should be combined in a bowl while the tempeh is steaming. After one minute, remove the tempeh from the saucepan and let it cool.
3. To drain any extra water, wrap the tempeh in a paper towel and softly press. The tempeh should then be cut into strips. (You need between 14 and 16 strips.)
4. Put the strips of tempeh in a small baking dish and cover with the marinade. Allow it to marinade for 10 minutes or more.
5. Set the temperature of the air fryer to 375°F or 190°C while the tempeh is marinating. In the air fryer, arrange the marinated tempeh in straight rows. Remaining marinade should be brushed onto the strips of tempeh. Cook the tempeh strips for 15 to 17 minutes, flipping them over halfway through.
6. Serve immediately and enjoy, or save for later.

Air fryer buffalo tempeh

Prep time : 20 mins
Cook time: 10 mins
Serving : 3

Ingredients

- 225 g Tempeh
- 1 tbsp white vinegar
- 68 ml almond milk plain
- 5 tbsp vegan butter

- 170 ml Red Hot or other hot suace
- 68 g cornstarch
- 64 g crush cornflakes or breadcrumbs
- 1/2 tsp garlic powder

Preparation Instructions :

1. Tempeh should be cut into 1/2 inch strips.
2. For at least 10 minutes, let the tempeh marinade in a container with 3 tbsp. red pepper flakes and vinegar. It's also possible to leave overnight.
3. Place crushed cornflakes, almond milk, and cornstarch in separate dishes.

4. Place each piece of the tempeh strip in the air fryer basket after coating it in cornstarch, almond milk, and cornflakes one at a time. Avoid crowding the air fryer, and keep the strips apart.

5. 375° F for 10 minutes in an air fryer to cook tempeh. To cook everything, you might need to cook in two batches.

6. Melted vegan butter, 1/2 cup red hot sauce, and garlic powder are combined to create buffalo sauce. Buffalo sauce can be used to dip or coat cooked tempeh strips. Enjoy!

Air fryer vegan buffalo tofu

Prep time : 15 mins
Cook time: 16 mins
Serving : 2-4

Ingredients

- 1 (225 g) container extra-firm tofu
- 4 tablespoons unsweetened rice milk
- ⅛ teaspoon garlic powder
- ⅛ teaspoon onion powder
- ⅔ cup vegan Buffalo wing sauce

- 4 tablespoons cornstarch
- 96 g panko bread crumbs
- ⅛ teaspoon paprika
- ⅛ teaspoon freshly ground black pepper

Preparation Instructions :

1. Take the tofu block out of the packaging and throw away the liquid. Tofu should be wrapped in cheesecloth, put on a platter, and covered with a heavy saucepan for about 10 minutes to press out any excess moisture. Tofu should be sliced into 20 1-inch, bite-sized pieces before the cheesecloth is removed. Place in a container that can be frozen, and freeze for eight hours or overnight.

2. Take the tofu out of the freezer and defrost it on some dry paper towels or cheesecloth. Clean off. Place cornstarch in a plastic bag that can be sealed while the tofu is defrosting. Put some rice milk in a small bowl. Set a 375°F air fryer temperature (190 degrees C).

3. Place the tofu in the cornstarch-filled bag, lock it, and shake to thoroughly cover the tofu pieces. Remove the tofu chunks, then cover them all with rice milk.

4. Place the cornstarch remnant in a resealable plastic bag along with the bread crumbs, garlic powder, paprika, onion powder, and pepper; shake to combine. Repackage the tofu in the bag with the bread crumbs, one piece at a time. Repeat with the remaining tofu pieces after shaking the bag until each piece is fully coated. Tap the bag lightly to remove any excess coating before setting the tofu on a wire rack.

5. In the air fryer basket, add coated tofu and cook for 10 minutes. To remove the fragments, shake the basket. 3 more minutes of cooking, or until browned.

6. Tofu bits that have been cooked should be placed in a bowl with 1/3 cup of Buffalo sauce. Then, continue tossing the tofu to evenly cover it with the remaining Buffalo sauce. Serve immediately.

Teriyaki Tofu

Prep time : 5 mins
Cook time: 10 mins
Serve 2

Ingredients

- 1 block extra firm tofu
- 56 g mirin
- 26 g soy sauce
- 8 g cornstarch
- 1 scallion, finely chopped
- 12 g granulated sugar
- 1 small garlic clove, grated (optional)

Preparation Instructions :

1. Tofu should be drained and paper towel wrapped. Leave for ten minutes. Slice the tofu into bite-sized chunks, averaging 1 to 1 1/2 inch squares, and remove the paper towel.
2. Combine the mirin, sugar, garlic, soy sauce, and a bowl. Till the sugar dissolves, continue stirring.
3. Put the teriyaki sauce in a storage bag and carefully transfer the tofu cubes there. Close the bag and gently shake the tofu and marinade until all the cubes are evenly covered. For 25 minutes, marinate.
4. Remove the tofu from the bag and arrange the cubes in a bowl carefully. The cornstarch should be sifted or sprinkled over the tofu, then it should be gently mixed with your fingers. Because sifting distributes the cornstarch more evenly.
5. After lightly misting the air fryer with cooking spray, add the tofu cubes, being sure to leave some room between each one.
6. Air fried for 9 to 11 minutes at 400 degrees Fahrenheit in the air fryer. Every two minutes or so, gently shake the tofu in the basket in the air fryer to prevent it from sticking to the bottom. When the tofu is golden brown, it is ready.
7. Serve the tofu on a platter with soy sauce drizzled over it and scallion that has been diced.

Air Fryer Spicy chickpeas

Prep time : 5 mins
Cook time: 20 mins
Serving : 4

Ingredients

- 1 (425 g) can chickpeas, rinsed and drained
- 1 tablespoon olive oil
- 1 teaspoon granulated garlic
- 1 pinch cumin
- 1 tablespoon nutritional yeast
- 1 teaspoon smoked paprika
- ½ teaspoon salt

Preparation Instructions :

1. Chickpeas should be spread out on two layers of paper towels, covered with another layer, and left to dry for 30 minutes.
2. Set air fryer to 355 degrees Fahrenheit (180 degrees C).
3. Toss together in a bowl: dried chickpeas, nutritional yeast, olive oil, smoked paprika, garlic, salt, and cumin.
4. Cook chickpeas in the air fryer for 20 to 22 minutes, stirring them every 4 minutes, until they are crispy.

Air Fryer green burger

Prep time : 80 mins
Cook time: 15 mins
Serving : 12

Ingredients

- 453 g Dry Chickpeas
- 1 Small Red Onion, quartered
- 85 g Fresh Parsley
- 21 g Loosely Packed Tarragon
- 1 Tablespoon Rice Vinegar
- 1 Teaspoon Ground Black Pepper
- 136 g Oat Flour
- 1/2 Teaspoon Baking Powder
- 1/2 Teaspoon Baking Soda
- 8 Cloves Garlic
- 43 gChopped Scallions
- 21 g Roughly Chopped Chives
- 2 Tablespoons Kosher Salt
- 1/2 Teaspoon Cayenne
- 2 Teaspoons Cornstarch
- GREEN DRESSING
- Toppings: spinach, tomatoes, pickles, pickled red onions
- 225 g Unsweetened Coconut Yogurt (or other non-dairy yogurt)

- 1 Tablespoon Chopped Parsley
- 1 Tablespoon Chopped Chives
- 1 Teaspoon Rice Vinegar
- Dash Cayenne

- 1 Tablespoon Chopped Tarragon
- 1 Teaspoon Lemon Juice
- 1 Teaspoon Garlic Powder
- Salt & Pepper, to taste

Preparation Instructions :

1. Soak the baking soda and chickpeas in warm water the day before you want to cook the burgers. Make careful to cover the beans with several inches of water since they will swell as they soak.
2. Add the rice vinegar, salt, pepper, cayenne, parsley, scallions, tarragon, chives, and chickpeas to a food processor. Mix until mostly smooth. Avoid overmixing.
3. Place the mixture in a basin and chill for about an hour.
4. Add the baking powder and oat flour after that. Create 1/2 cup patties out of the mixture. Place on the mesh tray of the air fryer after flattening.
5. Fry for 13–15 minutes on the third rack of the air fryer at 375 degrees. Make the green dressing in the meanwhile. In a small dish, combine all the dressing ingredients.
6. Put the burgers together once the patties are cooked. Then, top with your preferred toppings and a splash of green goddess dressing. Enjoy!

Air Fryer Bacon Wrapped Green Beans

Prep time : 15 mins
Cook time: 20 mins
Serving : 8

Ingredients
- cooking spray
- 1 (340 g) package bacon, strips cut in half
- 2 tablespoons brown sugar

- 1 (453 g) package frozen cut green beans
- salt and pepper to taste

Preparation Instructions :

1. Set air fryer to 355 degrees Fahrenheit (180 degrees C).
2. Lay out a half strip of bacon. Then, twist the bacon strip into a bundle. Place a tiny bunch of green beans (six or seven) on the bacon strip. Position the bundle seam-side down in the casserole. Repeat with the rest of the green beans and bacon slices. Put some salt, pepper, and brown sugar on top.
3. About 20 minutes into air frying, the food should be well-browned and cooked.

Air Fryer BBQ Lentil Meatballs

Prep time : 5 mins

Cook time: 40 mins
Serving : 3-5

Ingredients

- 680 g vegetable broth
- 43 g chopped dried mushrooms
- 85 g diced white or yellow onion
- 1 clove garlic, minced
- 3 tablespoons vegan BBQ sauce
- 1 tablespoon vegan Worcestershire sauce, or low-sodium soy sauce
- 1 teaspoon onion powder
- 1/2 teaspoon smoked paprika
- 1/4 teaspoon black pepper
- 340 g vegan BBQ sauce
- 85 g dry green or brown lentils
- 2 tablespoons avocado or sunflower oil
- 1 tablespoon tomato paste
- 68 g vital wheat gluten
- 2 tablespoons water or vegetable broth
- 1 teaspoon dried parsley
- 1/2 teaspoon salt, to taste
- Topping

Preparation Instructions :

1. Boil the lentils, mushrooms, and vegetable broth in a large saucepan over medium-high heat. Once liquid has been absorbed and the lentils are soft, reduce heat to medium-low and simmer for 20 minutes. Continue with the following step while the lentils are cooking.

2. Warm the oil in a small sauté pan over medium heat. Once the pan is heated, add the onions and cook for 7 to 10 minutes, or until the onions are beginning to caramelize. Next, reduce the heat to medium-low and add the garlic and tomato paste to the pan. After one more minute of sautéing, remove the pan.

3. Put cooked lentil/mushroom combination, onion/tomato mixture, essential wheat gluten, water, Worcestershire sauce, onion powder, parsley, smoked paprika, salt, and pepper in a food processor. You don't want a mushy hummus, so pulse just enough to blend the ingredients while keeping some chunks.

4. Spray a little cooking oil on the basket in your air fryer. Form two-tablespoon-sized lentil mixture balls after moistening your hands with water. With at least a half-inch between each ball, place them in the air fryer basket. It might be necessary to do this task in two batches depending on your air fryer.

5. The lentil balls should be lightly coated with cooking oil before being air-fried for 12 minutes at 350 degrees or until they are golden brown on the exterior. Place the lentil meatballs on a tray or platter, and then top with 1 cup of BBQ sauce. If you don't want the BBQ sauce to chill your balls down too much, you may reheat it in the microwave.) Serve with toothpicks and enjoy!

Air Fried Lentil Fritters

Prep time : 15 mins
Cook time: 30 mins
Serving : 3

Ingredients

- Ingredients for Air Fried Lentil Fritters
- 43 g Onions , (sliced)
- 1 tablespoon Ginger garlic paste
- 1 teaspoon Red chili powder
- ½ teaspoon Cumin powder
- 21 g Mint leaves , (chopped)
- 1 teaspoon Salt
- Ingredients for the Tamarind Mint chutney
- 2 tablespoon Tamarind
- 2 teaspoon Salt
- 136 g Besan
- 1 tablespoon Green chilies , (chopped)
- ½ teaspoon Turmeric powder
- 1 teaspoon Coriander powder
- ½ teaspoon Garam masala powder
- 43 g Red lentil or Masoor Dal, (boiled)
- 340 ml Water , (optional)
- 1 bunch Mint leaves
- 3-5 pcs Green chilies

Preparation Instructions :

1. For five minutes, pre-heat the air fryer at 400 degrees. All the ingredients for the pakodas should be combined thoroughly in a mixing basin. To form a thick paste, gradually add water as needed. If the dal has water, do not add any extra water.
2. Spray oil on the air fryer basket. The next step is to add a lump of the prepared mixture to the air fryer basket. Make as many lumps as you can in the meanwhile. Be careful not to make them too big or the middle won't be cooked through.
3. They should be sprayed with some oil and cooked for 10 to 15 minutes at 400 degrees.
4. To assure that they are cooked properly, you may turn them once in between and spray some oil on them.
5. Blend all of the ingredients for the tamarind chutney in a blender. If necessary, adjust the salt and tamarind.
6. Red lentil pakodas make a delightful snack when served hot with tamarind chutney and tea.

Air Fried Butter Beans

Prep time : 3 mins
Cook time: 15mins
Serving : 4

Ingredients

- 439 g butter beans 1 can
- 1 tsp garlic powder
- ½ tsp cumin powder
- 1 tbsp olive oil
- 1 tsp onion powder
- kosher salt

Preparation Instructions :

1. Your air fryer should be preheated to 370 degrees.
2. Butter beans should be drained, spread out on a piece of paper towel, and patted dry.
3. Put your beans in a big bowl and add salt and spices to taste.
4. Your beans should be spread out in a single layer and cooked for 10 to 15 minutes in the air

fryer basket (tossing them once halfway through the cooking time.)

5. Check your beans after 10 minutes. If you like them extra crispy, cook them for an additional 5 minutes.

Kidney Bean "Popcorn"

Prep time : 5 mins
Cook time: 25 mins
Serving : 2

Ingredients

- 1 (1425 g) can kidney beans, drained and rinsed
- olive oil cooking spray
- 1 teaspoon sea salt, or to taste

Preparation Instructions :

1. Set an air fryer at 325 degrees Fahrenheit (165 degrees C)
2. Sea salt should be added after spraying olive oil cooking spray on the kidney beans. Spread out in the air fryer basket in a single layer.
3. Cook the kidney beans in the air fryer for 25 to 30 minutes, or until they have all cracked open and turned crunchy. If they appear under-toasted, air-fry them for an additional five minutes; they should all have different shades of brown.
4. Allow to cool before storing in a sandwich bag or airtight container.

Black Bean Chimichangas

Prep time : 20 mins
Cook time: 5 mins
Serving : 6

Ingredients

- 2 cans (425 g each) black beans, rinsed and drained
- 1 package (250 g) ready-to-serve brown rice
- 134 g frozen corn
- 134 g minced fresh cilantro
- 1/2 teaspoon salt
- 4 teaspoons olive oil
- 134 g chopped green onions
- 6 whole wheat tortillas (8 inches), warmed if necessary
- Optional: Guacamole and salsa

Preparation Instructions :

1. Set the air fryer to 400°. Beans, rice, and corn should all be combined in a large microwave-safe dish. Microwave the mixture, covered, for 4-5 minutes, stirring halfway through. Add the

salt, green onions, and cilantro.

2. To assemble, spread each tortilla's center with 3/4 cup of the bean mixture. Over the filling, fold the tortilla's bottom and sides, then roll it up. olive oil for brushing

3. Place oiled trays in the air fryer basket in batches, seam side down. 2-3 minutes or until crispy and golden brown. Serve alongside salsa and guacamole, if preferred.

Black Bean Burgers

Prep time : 20 mins
Cook time: 10 mins
Serving : 4

Ingredients

- 1 (425 g) can black beans, drained, rinsed, and patted dry
- 1 tablespoon extra-virgin olive oil
- 64 g finely chopped sweet pepper
- 1/2 teaspoon paprika
- 1 teaspoon ground cumin
- 2 tablespoons barbecue sauce
- 1 large egg (use flax egg if vegan*)
- Nonstick cooking spray
- 64 g finely chopped yellow onion
- 2 cloves garlic, minced
- 1 teaspoon chili powder
- 1/4 teaspoon cayenne pepper (optional)
- 50 g, plus 2 tablespoons breadcrumbs
- Salt and pepper to taste
- Warmed buns and desired toppings (sliced cheese, tomatoes, lettuce, onion, barbecue sauce, etc.)

Preparation Instructions :

1. Set the oven to 350°F. Spread beans in a single layer on a small baking sheet that has been lined with parchment paper. Bake beans for 10 to 12 minutes at 350°F, or until barely dry. Let it cool.

2. In a little skillet over medium-high heat, warm the olive oil. Add the onion and pepper, and cook for 3 to 4 minutes, until soft. Once aromatic, add the garlic and continue to cook for 1 more minute.

3. Vegetables should be pressed gently to drain away moisture after being scraped into a fine-mesh sieve. Place aside.

4. Use a fork to gently mash the beans into a paste in a large bowl (you want some pieces). Stir in the veggies, breadcrumbs, egg, barbecue sauce, paprika, chili powder, cumin, cayenne pepper, and salt & pepper to taste. Black bean mixture should be gently folded until just combined.

5. Make 4 patties out of the black bean mixture. Wrap tightly and keep chilled until needed (patties may be refrigerated up to 4 days and frozen up to 1 month)

6. When ready to cook, oil the grate of a 4-qt air fryer with nonstick cooking spray and warm to 375F. Lay patties in a single layer and air fry at 375F for 6 minutes, turning burgers midway through cooking (we usually cook 2 at a time in our 6-qt).

7. Burgers should be taken out of the air fryer and served warm with chosen toppings on buns. Enjoy!

Air Fryer crunchy green peas

Prep time : 20 mins
Cook time: 8 mins
Serving : 4

Ingredients

- 250 g frozen green peas, thawed
- 1/2 teaspoon salt
- 1/4 teaspoon smoked paprika
- 1-2 tablespoons olive oil
- 1/2 teaspoon garlic powder

Preparation Instructions :

1. Like crispy chickpeas, the secret to achieving crispy air-fried green peas is to dry them off and squeeze as much moisture out of the peas as you can.
2. To let them dry, spread them out on a kitchen towel or some paper towels. It won't take more than ten to fifteen minutes.
3. Salt, garlic powder, smoked paprika, and olive oil should all be added.
4. Check that the green peas are completely covered. (This is another another tip for obtaining really crispy green peas.)
5. Then spread the peas inside the air fryer basket and warm your air fryer to 350 degrees F. While shaking the basket often, set the timer for 8 to 10 minutes. To flip them halfway in an air fryer oven, use a pair of tongs.
6. Transfer to a container that is airtight.

Air Fryer Broccolini Salad with lentils

Prep time : 5 mins
Cook time: 7 mins
Serving : 2-4

Ingredients

- 2 bunches broccolini
- Olive oil cooking spray
- 2 handfuls baby spinach leaves
- 2 tablespoons toasted almond flakes
- 2 tablespoons tahini
- 1–2 tablespoons lemon juice
- Salt + pepper
- 1 can brown lentils
- 32 g dried cranberries
- Hot honey tahini Dressing:
- 2 teaspoons hot honey
- Salt + pepper, to taste

Preparation Instructions :

1. After washing the broccolini, blot it dry with paper towels. Cut off the ends.
2. Olive oil, salt, and pepper should be tossed with the broccolini stems.
3. Broccoli should be added to a baking paper-lined air fryer basket. To ensure equal cooking, air fried the food for 8–10 minutes at 180°C/350°F while checking and stirring the basket every 3–4 minutes.
4. Put the tahini, warm honey, lemon juice, water, salt, and pepper in a bowl. If necessary, add more water to thin.
5. Baby spinach leaves, cooked broccolini, lentils, cranberries, and toasted almonds should all be combined in a big bowl or serving dish.
6. Enjoy the tahini dressing once you pour it over.

Air Fryer Pesto Salmon with Lentil Salad

Prep time : 20 mins

Cook time: 25 mins

Serving : 4

Ingredients

- 4 (141 g) skin-on salmon fillets
- 1 tsp. black pepper, divided
- 2 Tbsp. red wine vinegar
- 2 Tbsp. fresh lemon juice, plus 1 lemon, cut into wedges
- 1 Tbsp. Dijon mustard
- 2 (400g) cans lentils, drained and rinsed
- 21 g chopped fresh flat-leaf parsley
- 170 g jarred basil pesto
- 1 ½ tsp. kosher salt, divided
- Cooking spray
- 8 Tbsp. extra-virgin olive oil, divided
- 96 g chopped red onion
- 340 g packed baby arugula

Preparation Instructions :

1. For 3 minutes, heat the air fryer to 375 degrees. One teaspoon of salt and one-half teaspoon of pepper should be distributed evenly over the fish. Apply cooking spray generously to the air fryer basket. Salmon should be added to the basket with the skin side facing down. Cook for 9 minutes or until salmon is golden brown, flaky, and a thermometer placed in the middle of the fillets reads 145°.
2. In the meantime, combine 6 tablespoons of the olive oil, the mustard, lemon juice, and vinegar in a big bowl. Add the remaining 12 teaspoon each of salt and pepper, along with the lentils, onion, and parsley. Fold in the arugula and set aside. In a separate small dish, combine the pesto and the remaining 2 tablespoons of olive oil.
3. On top of or next to the salad, arrange the salmon fillets on each of the four dishes. Over the salmon, spoon the pesto mixture evenly. Lemon wedges are recommended.

Pesto Baby Potatoes

Prep time : 5 mins
Cook time: 18 mins
Serving : 5

Ingredients

- 680 g Baby Potatoes, cut in half
- ½ tsp. Sea Salt
- 170 g Pesto or my Gluten Free Homemade Walnut Pesto Recipe
- 43 g Parmesan Cheese, grated
- 2 Tbsp. Avocado Oil
- ¼ tsp. Coarse Ground Black Pepper

Preparation Instructions :

1. After washing, cut each baby potato in half. You might need to chop the young potatoes into quarters if any of them are significantly larger than the rest. To ensure consistent cooking, the potato chunks must be around the same size.
2. Sliced baby potatoes, avocado oil, salt, and pepper should all be combined in a big bowl. Mix to evenly distribute oil and spice on the potatoes.
3. Fill the Ninja foodi air fryer basket evenly with the potato mixture. 12–15 minutes of air frying at 390 degrees. To ensure that all of the potatoes brown, shake the air fryer basket once or twice midway through cooking. Air fry for an additional 2 to 3 minutes if necessary.
4. Return the warm potatoes to the big dish. Add the grated parmesan cheese and pesto. To melt the cheese and coat the potatoes, stir the mixture.
5. Serve warm or cold right away.

Air Fryer Spaghetti Bolognese sauce

Cook time: 40 mins
Serving : 2

Ingredients

- 227 grams lean beef
- 28 grams carrot
- 1 clove garlic, minced
- 397 grams can crushed tomatoes
- ½ tablespoon dried oregano
- salt and pepper, to taste
- cooked whole grain pasta or spaghetti squash, for serving
- 2 tablespoons grated Parmesan cheese (omit for dairy-free)
- 85 grams onion
- 28 grams stalk celery
- 1 tablespoon olive oil
- ½ tablespoon dried parsley
- ½ tablespoon dried basil

• 2 tablespoons fresh basil leaves (for garnish)

Preparation Instructions :

1. As finely as you can, crumble the raw ground beef. It won't fully cook if you leave it in large bits.
2. Onion into 1-inch dice and mince the garlic (1.27 cm). The celery and carrot should be diced into 14-inch (0.6 cm) or smaller pieces. The celery and carrots must be extremely finely chopped in order to cook more quickly.
3. The air fryer should be preheated for 5 minutes at 375°F (190°C).
4. Carefully place the ground beef on roughly half of an air fryer tray that has been heated. The other half of the tray should be covered with the onions, celery, carrots, and garlic. olive oil over the vegetables. The air fryer oven's top rack should be where you place the tray.
5. 375°F (190°C) for 5 minutes of air frying. If necessary, finely crumble the ground meat. The sauce won't make the carrots and celery any softer. If necessary, air fried them for a few more minutes.
6. Parchment paper should be used to line an aluminum pan that is 8 by 8 inches (20.3 by 20.3 cm). Place the pan with the cooked meat and vegetables. Crushed tomatoes, dried basil, oregano, parsley, and salt and pepper should all be added. Stir.
7. Wrap foil firmly around the pan. Place on a rack in the center of the air fryer, and air fried for 35–45 minutes at 375°F (190°C). Give the sauce five minutes to cool.
8. Serve your preferred spaghetti or spiralized vegetables with the bolognese sauce. Top with Parmesan cheese and fresh basil, if desired.

Air Fryer No Knead Bread

Prep time : 10 mins
Cook time: 30 mins
Serving : 6

Ingredients

• 204 g all-purpose flour
• 1 teaspoon instant yeast
• 1 teaspoon salt
• 255 ml water room temperature

Preparation Instructions :

1. Mix the flour, salt, instant yeast, and water in a large bowl using a wooden spoon or spatula until everything is thoroughly combined. It will be shaggy and sticky dough.
2. The bowl should be covered with plastic wrap and left to set for two to three hours on your counter or in your unheated oven. During this time, the dough should double in size.
3. Put a 6-inch circular pan in the air fryer's basket. With the pan inside, heat the air fryer to 400°F for 20 minutes.
4. While waiting, carefully flour your hands and lightly dust the dough with flour. The dough should be carefully removed from the bowl using floured hands, and it should be roughly

shaped into a ball. Place the dough ball over a sheet of parchment paper after grabbing it. Once the pan has been heated, place the dough and parchment paper in a bowl and cover with a dry, clean dish towel. Lift the parchment paper carefully and place it in the pot after carefully removing the pan from the air fryer basked. A sharp knife can also be used to cut slits in the dough's top. Your bread will look nice and maybe stay from breaking if you do this. Re-insert the pan into the air fryer basket, secure the edges with aluminum foil, and then bake for a specified amount of time.

5. After 20 minutes of baking the bread, carefully remove the foil by opening the basket. Seal the basket and bake for a further 10 minutes, or until golden. If you tap the bread, it is done when it makes a hollow sound. The bread was turned upside down after 5 minutes to enable the bottom to brown as well although this step is entirely optional.

Air Fryer Pasta chips

Prep time : 15 mins
Cook time: 10 mins
Serving : 2

Ingredients

- 225 g rigatoni noodles, cooked al dente and drained
- 1 teaspoon garlic, minced
- ½ teaspoon black pepper
- 3 tablespoons olive oil, divided
- 1 teaspoon kosher salt
- 43 g parmesan cheese, grated

Preparation Instructions :

1. heat the air fryer to 400 degrees.
2. Add cooked noodles to a big bowl. 1 tablespoon of olive oil should be drizzled on. Coat by tossing.
3. Place the spaghetti noodles in a single layer on the rack or basket of the air fryer.
4. 8 to 10 minutes, or until golden brown, in the air fryer.
5. Pasta chips should be placed in a bowl.
6. Combine the remaining oil, garlic, salt, and pepper in a separate bowl. Mix thoroughly.
7. Toss the spaghetti chips in the oil mixture to coat.
8. Serve with your preferred dipping sauce, such as marinara or garlic sauce, and sprinkle with parmesan Parmesan.

Air Fryer fried rice

Prep time : 10 mins
Cook time: 15 mins
Serving : 4

Ingredients

- 2 tbsp unsalted butter, melted
- 2 large eggs, cooked and scrambled

- 128 g frozen mixed vegetables, no need to thaw
- 3 cloves garlic, minced
- 384 g cooked and chilled rice, can use either white or brown rice
- 2 tbsp low sodium soy sauce
- 1 tsp sesame oil
- 1 small onion, diced
- 1 tbsp oyster sauce
- green onions for garnish, if desired

Preparation Instructions :

1. Turn the air fryer on to 350 degrees. In the meantime, combine the melted butter with the cooked eggs, onion, garlic, cooked rice, frozen mixed veggies, soy sauce, oyster sauce, and sesame oil in a skillet that may be placed in the oven. I made use of an 8 x 3 cake pan.
2. Stirring should be done every five minutes during cooking for 10-15 minutes.
3. Remove the rice and vegetables from the air fryer once they are cooked, then serve them right away with green onions as a garnish, if preferred.

Air Fryer garlic bread

Prep time : 5 mins
Cook time: 5 mins
Serving : 4

Ingredients

- ½ loaf Italian or french bread
- ½ tablespoon minced fresh parsley (or use 1 teaspoon dried parsley)
- 4 tablespoons unsalted butter, room temperature
- 2 large cloves garlic, minced
- ¼ teaspoon salt (or as needed)

Preparation Instructions :

1. Split a French or Italian loaf in half horizontally and then in half lengthwise.
2. To make garlic butter, put the butter, garlic, parsley, and salt in a small bowl and stir to blend.
3. Butter mixture should be applied to both halves.
4. 5 minutes of 350° F preheating the air fryer. Cook the bread, butter side up, until it becomes golden. (If after five minutes the bread still doesn't become golden, fry it for a few more seconds at the same temperature.)
4. HOT SERVE!

Mac and Cheese

Prep time : 5 mins
Cook time: 20 mins
Serving : 4

Ingredients

- 192 g elbow macaroni
- 170 g heavy cream
- 1 teaspoon dry mustard
- ½ teaspoon black pepper
- 236 ml water
- 226 g sharp cheddar cheese shredded and separated
- ½ teaspoon kosher salt
- 1/4 teaspoon garlic powder

Preparation Instructions :

1. In a 7-inch pan with enough thickness to fit all the ingredients, mix elbow macaroni, water, heavy cream, 34 of the cheese, dry mustard, kosher salt, black pepper, and garlic powder. Stir to combine.

2. Set the Ninja foodi Air Fryer to 360 degrees Fahrenheit and place in the basket. Start the Air Fryer and set the timer for 18 to 20 minutes. Open the Air Fryer basket halfway through frying, add the remaining cheese, and mix. Close the door and keep cooking.

3. Open the Air Fryer once the food has finished cooking and mix the mac and cheese. After removing the pan from the basket, let it cool for five to ten minutes. While it cools, the mac and cheese will thicken. Enjoy and Serve

Loaded-Pizza Baked Potatoes

Prep time : 20 mins
Cook time: 50 mins
Serving : 4

Ingredients

- 4 medium russet potatoes
- 1/2 teaspoon kosher salt
- 1/2 medium green bell pepper, chopped
- 170 g marinara sauce
- 85 g finely shredded low-moisture part-skim mozzarella cheese
- 21 g grated Parmesan cheese
- 1 tablespoon unsalted butter, melted
- 2 slices applewood smoked uncured bacon, chopped
- 1 baby bella mushroom, thinly sliced

- 2 teaspoons fresh chopped basil

Preparation Instructions :

1. Pre-heat ninja foodi ffor 5 minutes at 400 degrees. Sprinkle salt over potatoes after buttering them. Place potatoes in the air fryer and cook for 40 minutes at 400 degrees, or until a knife can be easily inserted.

2.In a small pan, fry the bacon for 5 minutes over medium-high heat, turning periodically. Then, using a slotted spoon, move the bacon to a plate lined with paper towels. Cook pepper and mushroom for 5 minutes, or until they are tender-crisp, in the same pan with the drippings.

3. Make a 4-inch slit in the top of each potato, then stuff with mozzarella, Parmesan, marinara, and the pepper mixture. If required, cook the potatoes in 2 batches in the air fryer for 5 minutes at 400 degrees, or until golden brown and the cheese has melted.

4. Serve potatoes with bacon and basil leaves.

Air Fryer Pizza

Prep time : 5 mins
Cook time: 7 mins
Serving : 2

Ingredients

- Buffalo mozzarella
- Olive oil
- Pizza dough 1 12-inch dough will make 2 personal sized pizzas
- Tomato sauce
- Optional toppings to finish: fresh basil, parmesan cheese, pepper flakes

Preparation Instructions :

1. Turn on Ninja foodi air fryer and heat to 375°F (190°C). Oil the air fryer basket well. Use paper towels to dry the mozzarella (to prevent a soggy pizza).
2. Roll out the pizza dough to fit the air fryer basket. Transfer it carefully to the air fryer, then lightly spray it with a teaspoon or so of olive oil. 3 minutes of cooking.
3. Spoon a thin layer of tomato sauce and buffalo mozzarella pieces onto the precooked dough.
4. about 7 minutes, or until cheese has melted and the crust is crispy. Just before serving, you may add basil, grated parmesan, and pepper flakes as a topping.

Air Fryer Pasta Bake

Prep time : 20 mins
Cook time: 25 mins
Serving : 2

Ingredients

- 1 tablespoon oil (for cooking)
- 1 red bell pepper (diced)
- 225g ground turkey (or any other ground meat)
- 235ml pasta sauce (I used marinara)
- 1 onion (diced)
- salt and pepper
- 170g pasta (I used rigatoni)
- 4 tablespoons shredded cheese

Preparation Instructions :

1. Follow the directions on the pasta package for cooking. Drain, then set apart. While the pasta is cooking, you can prep the rest of the dish.
2. In a skillet over medium-high heat, warm the oil. Once it's heated, add the bell pepper and onion, and simmer until tender. Add the ground turkey and heat until browned. Season with salt and pepper.
3. Spaghetti that has been cooked and pasta sauce are added and combined. Turn the heat off.
4. The ninja foodi air fryer should be heated to 360F.
5. Transfer the sauce and pasta to an air fryer-compatible baking dish that is oven-safe. Add the cheese shavings on top.

6. For seven to nine minutes, air fried the pasta.

Air Fryer Pasta Bake

Prep time : 10 mins
Cook time: 10 mins
Serving : 2

Ingredients

- 152 g dry whole wheat bow tie pasta
- 1 tbsp 7 g nutritional yeast
- 1/2 tsp salt
- 1 tbsp 15 ml olive oil
- 1 1/2 tsp 3 g Italian Seasoning Blend

Preparation Instructions :

1. Pasta should be cooked for only half the time specified on the package.
2. Combine the drained pasta with the salt, nutritional yeast, olive oil, and Italian seasoning.
3. Put everything at once in your ninja foodi air fryer.
4. Cook for five minutes at 390°F (200°C). Cook for a further 3 to 5 minutes, or until crispy, after shaking the basket. (As they cool, they will become more crisp.)

Air Fryer tortilla Pizza

Prep time : 5 mins
Cook time: 10 mins
Serving : 1

Ingredients

- 1 flour tortilla (6-8-inch size)
- 30 ml shredded cheese
- black pepper , to taste
- 45 ml pizza sauce or salsa
- salt , to taste
- OPTIONAL TOPPINGS
- Diced Tomatoes, Mushrooms or Pepperoni, cooked Sausage, Bacon pieces, red onion, black beans, sliced.
- OTHER SAUCE OPTIONS
- BBQ Sauce, Salsa, White (Alfredo) Sauce, Pesto, etc.

Preparation Instructions :

1. Insert the tortilla into the air fryer. Air Fry at 360°F/182°C about 2-3 minutes or until the tortilla is almost crispy.
2. Flip the tortilla. Cover the tortilla with the sauce. Add cheese, more salt, pepper, and any other desired toppings before topping.
3. A rack for an air fryer should be placed above the tortilla pizza to prevent the topping from floating about.
4. For 2 to 5 minutes, or until cooked through and the cheese has melted, air fry the pizza at 360°F/182°C.

Air fryer Fresh fruit

Prep time : 5 mins

Cook time: 8 mins

Serving : 4

Ingredients

- 128 g fresh pineapple cut into bite sized pieces
- 128 g mango cut into bite sized pieces
- 128 g apricot chunks cut into bite sized pieces
- Glaze
- 110 brown sugar
- 170 l orange juice
- ¼ teaspoon cinnamon

Preparation Instructions :

1. Fruit should be cut into bite-size pieces.
2. Brown sugar, orange juice, and cinnamon should all be thoroughly blended.
3. Give the fruit a good layer of glaze.
4. For five minutes, heat the air fryer to 390°F/198°C.
5. Spray the air fryer basket lightly. Cook the fruit for 4 minutes after adding it to the basket.
6. Stir the fruit around. Cook for an extra 4 minutes if you'd want it to be done more thoroughly, and spritz with oil if you'd like.
7. Carefully remove from the air fryer basket and enjoy! Add chopped nuts or coconut as an optional garnish.

Caramelized stone fruit

Prep time : 3 mins

Cook time: 15 mins

Serving : 2

Ingredients

- 2-3 stone fruits such as peaches, nectarines, plums or apricots
- 1 tbsp Maple syrup
- 1/2 tbsp tbsp Coconut sugar
- 1/4 tsp Cinnamon, optional
- pinch of salt, optional

Preparation Instructions :

1. Place a parchment paper sheet into your air fryer basket after cutting it to suit the bottom of the basket.
2. Remove the seed by cutting the stone fruit in half. Next, apply some maple syrup with a brush on the flesh and top with some coconut sugar. If desired, include a pinch of salt and cinnamon.
3. In the air fryer basket, add the stone fruit, and air fried at 350 degrees for 15 minutes, or until caramelized.

Apple Fries

Prep time : 20 mins
Cook time: 8 mins
Serving : 8

Ingredients

Apple Fries Ingredients:

- 3 large apples
- 170 g graham cracker crumbs
- 3 large eggs
- 100 g granulated sugar

Caramel Apple Dip :

- 100 g granulated sugar
- 1/2 teaspoon salt
- 110 g brown sugar
- 1 teaspoon pure vanilla extract
- 225 g room temperature cream cheese

Preparation Instructions :

1. Spray some olive oil in the basket of your air fryer.
2. The apples should first be peeled before being sliced into wedges.
3. Combine the sugar and graham crackers in a small mixing basin.
4. Break the eggs into a second, smaller bowl, and whisk them to combine them.
5. Before placing them in the graham cracker mixture, dip the apples in the egg mixture. (After each dip, shake to get rid of any excess.)
6. Place the apples in the oiled air fryer basket as you coat them.
7. Once you've finished coating the apples, liberally mist them with olive oil to help them crisp up.
8. Set the temperature to 380 degrees F, air fryer setting, for 8 to 10 minutes. Using tongs, turn the apple fries halfway through cooking. Spray them lightly with olive oil once you've turned them over.
9. Enjoy after plating and serving!

Air fryer Pineapple

Prep time : 5 mins
Cook time: 10 mins
Serving : 4

Ingredients

- 1 large pineapple sliced
- 4 tablespoons butter melted
- 220 g brown sugar
- 2 teaspoons ground cinnamon

Preparation Instructions :

1. Combine the butter, brown sugar, and ground cinnamon in a small bowl.
2. Apply a light coating with a pastry brush to the pineapple.
3. Put the tray into the air fryer and set the temperature to 250 degrees F for 5 minutes; after that, Upped it to 400 degrees F for 5 minutes to obtain a roasting taste.
4. Serve, plate, and have fun!
5. Enjoy after plating and serving!

Air fryer Bananas

Prep time : 5 mins
Cook time: 8 mins
Serving : 8

Ingredients

- 1 banana
- 2 tablespoon sugar
- 1 teaspoon ground cinnamon
- 1 tablespoon rolled oats
- Optional, For Serving: 1/2 teaspoon sparkling sugar
- Cooking Spray

Preparation Instructions :

1. Bananas should be cut into thin slices and then placed on an air fryer pan that has been coated with nonstick or olive oil cooking spray.
2. Then combine the sugar, cinnamon powder, and rolled oats in a small bowl.
3. Bananas are dipped in the mixture. Then, set your air fryer to the air fryer setting at 400 degrees F for 4 to 8 minutes. Before serving, sprinkle with sparkling sugar.
4. Enjoy! Plate and serve!

Air fryer Garlic-Herb Fried Patty Pan Squash

Cook time: 25 mins
Serving : 4

Ingredients

- 640 g halved small pattypan squash
- 1 tablespoon olive oil

- 2 garlic cloves, minced
- 1/4 teaspoon dried oregano
- 1/4 teaspoon pepper
- 1/2 teaspoon salt
- 1/4 teaspoon dried thyme
- 1 tablespoon minced fresh parsley

Preparation Instructions :

1. Set the air fryer to 375 degrees.
2. Put the squash in a big bowl. Drizzle squash with a mixture of oil, garlic, salt, oregano, thyme, and pepper.
3. Toss to coat. Place the squash in the air fryer basket on the oiled tray.
4. Cook for 10 to 15 minutes, stirring occasionally, until soft. Add some parsley.

Beets with Orange Gremolata and Goat Cheese

Prep: 25 min
Cook time: 40 mins
Serving : 12

Ingredients

- 3 medium fresh golden beets (450 g)
- 1 garlic clove, minced
- 3 tablespoons crumbled goat cheese
- 2 tablespoons lime juice
- 1/2 teaspoon fine sea salt
- 1 tablespoon minced fresh sage
- 3 medium fresh beets (about 450 g)
- 1 teaspoon grated orange zest
- 2 tablespoons sunflower kernels
- 2 tablespoons orange juice
- 1 tablespoon minced fresh parsley

Preparation Instructions :

1. Preheat air fryer to 400°. Beets should be cleaned, and the tops should be cut off by one inch. Beets should be placed on double-thick heavy-duty foil (about 24x12 in.).
2. Beets are wrapped in foil and sealed firmly. Place on tray in Ninja foodi air fryer basket in a single layer. Cook for 45 to 55 minutes, until tender. To let steam out, carefully open the foil.
3. Peel, cut in half, and slice the beets when they are cold enough to handle; arrange in a serving bowl. Add salt, lime juice, and orange juice; mix to combine.
4. Sprinkle the beets with a mixture of parsley, sage, garlic, and orange zest. Add goat cheese and sunflower kernels on top. Serve hot or cold.

Fried Avocado Tacos

Prep: 30 min
Cook time: 10 mins
Serving : 4

Ingredients

- 170 g shredded fresh kale or coleslaw mix
- 85 g cup plain Greek yogurt
- 1 teaspoon honey
- 1/4 teaspoon ground chipotle pepper
- 21 g minced fresh cilantro
- 2 tablespoons lime juice
- 1/4 teaspoon salt
- 1/4 teaspoon pepper

TACOS INGREDIENTS:

- 1 large egg, beaten
- 1/2 teaspoon salt
- 1/2 teaspoon ground chipotle pepper
- Cooking spray
- 1 medium tomato, chopped
- 32 g cornmeal
- 1/2 teaspoon garlic powder
- 2 medium avocados, peeled and sliced
- 8 flour tortillas or corn tortillas (6 inches)
- Crumbled queso fresco, optional

Preparation Instructions :

1. In a bowl, mix the first 8 ingredients. Keep chilled until serving, covered.
2. Set the air fryer to 400 degrees. Egg should be put in a small bowl. Combine cornmeal, salt, garlic powder, and chipotle pepper in a separate shallow basin. Avocado slices should be dipped in egg, then lightly patted into a cornmeal mixture to help them adhere.
3. Avocado slices should be placed in single layers on a greased tray in the Ninja Foodi air fryer basket and sprayed with cooking spray as you go. Cook for 4 minutes or until golden brown. Toss with cooking spray and turn. Cook for 3–4 more minutes, or until golden brown.
4. Avocado slices should be served in tortillas along with kale mixture, tomato, more chopped cilantro, and, if preferred, queso fresco.

Portobello Melts

total time: 25 mins
Serving : 2

Ingredients

- 2 large portobello mushrooms (113 g each), stems removed
- 85 ml olive oil
- 1/2 teaspoon salt
- 4 tomato slices
- 2 slices Italian bread (1 inch thick)
- 2 tablespoons balsamic vinegar
- 1/2 teaspoon dried basil
- 2 slices mozzarella cheese
- Chopped fresh basil

Preparation Instructions :

1. Prepare a small bowl and add the mushrooms. Brush the mixture of oil, vinegar, salt, and dried basil on the undersides of the mushrooms. Wait for five minutes. Save any leftover marinade. the air fryer to 400 degrees.
2. Place the stem side of the mushrooms in the air fryer basket on the oiled tray. Cook until tender, 3-4 minutes per side.
3. Take out of the basket. Add tomato and cheese to the stem sides and secure with toothpicks.

Cook until cheese is melted, about 1 minute. Take out and keep heated; throw away the toothpicks.

4. Brush saved marinade on bread before placing it on the tray in the air fryer basket. Cook for 2 to 3 minutes, until gently toasted. Add mushrooms on top. Add some chopped basil on top.

Pumpkin Fries

Prep: 25 min
Cook: 15 min./batch
Serving : 4

Ingredients

- 170 g plain Greek yogurt
- 2 tablespoons maple syrup
- 2 to 3 teaspoons minced chipotle peppers in adobo sauce
- 1/8 teaspoon plus 1/2 teaspoon salt, divided
- 1/4 teaspoon ground cumin
- 1/4 teaspoon chili powder
- 1/4 teaspoon pepper
- 1 medium pie pumpkin
- 1/4 teaspoon garlic powder

Preparation Instructions :

1. Yogurt, maple syrup, chipotle peppers, and 1/8 teaspoon salt are combined in a small bowl. Keep chilled until serving.
2. Set the air fryer to 400 degrees.
3. Pumpkin should be peeled and chopped lengthwise. Save seeds for toasting or throw them away. pumpkin into 1/2-inch pieces. strips. Place in a large bowl. Add the remaining half teaspoon of salt, along with the cumin, chili powder, garlic powder, and pepper, and toss to coat.
4. Place the pumpkin in the air fryer basket in batches on an oiled tray. Cook for 6 to 8 minutes, or until barely tender. Cook for an another 3 to 5 minutes, stirring to distribute the ingredients. Serve with sauce.

Herb and Lemon Cauliflower

Prep: 25 min
Cook: 15 min./batch
Serving : 4

Ingredients

- 1 medium head cauliflower, cut into florets (about 760 g)
- 4 tablespoons olive oil, divided
- 21 g minced fresh parsley
- 1 tablespoon minced fresh rosemary

- 1 tablespoon minced fresh thyme
- 1 teaspoon grated lemon zest
- 2 tablespoons lemon juice
- 1/2 teaspoon salt
- 1/4 teaspoon crushed red pepper flakes

Preparation Instructions :

1. Set the air fryer to 350 degrees. Cauliflower and 2 tablespoons of olive oil are combined in a large bowl and coated.
2. Cauliflower should be placed in a single layer in the air fryer basket on a tray in batches. Cook for 8 to 10 minutes, stirring halfway through, or until the edges are browned and the florets are soft.
3. Add the remaining ingredients and 2 tablespoons of oil to a small bowl. Transfer the cauliflower to a big bowl, adding the herb mixture and mixing well.

Mushroom Roll-Ups

Prep: 30 min
Cook: 10 min./batch
Serving : makes 10

Ingredients

- 2 tablespoons extra virgin olive oil
- 225 g large portobello mushrooms, gills discarded, finely chopped
- 1 teaspoon dried oregano
- 1/2 teaspoon crushed red pepper flakes
- 1 package (8 ounces) cream cheese, softened
- 10 flour tortillas (8 inches)
- Chutney
- 1 teaspoon dried thyme
- 1/4 teaspoon salt
- 113 g whole-milk ricotta cheese
- Cooking spray

Preparation Instructions :

1. Heat oil in a skillet over a medium heat. Add the mushrooms and cook for 4 minutes. Add salt, pepper flakes, oregano, and thyme. Sauté for 4-6 minutes, or until mushrooms are browned. Cool.
2. Combine the cheeses, then thoroughly fold in the mushrooms.
3. Place 3 tablespoons of the mushroom mixture in the middle of each tortilla's bottom. Roll firmly, then use toothpicks to fasten.
4. Set the air fryer to 400 degrees. Place roll-ups in the air fryer basket in batches on a greased tray and spritz with cooking spray.
5. Cook for 9 to 11 minutes or until golden brown. Discard toothpicks once roll-ups have cooled enough to handle. Chutney is suggested.

Nuts and bolts

Prep: 10 min
Cook: 25 min./batch
Serving : 4

Ingredients

- 450 g dried farfalle pasta
- 2 tbsp brown sugar
- 1 tsp onion powder
- 1/2 tsp chilli powder
- 80 g raw macadamias
- 227 g Kellog's Nutri-grain cereal
- 60ml extra virgin olive oil
- 2 tsp smoked paprika
- 1/2 tsp garlic powder
- 1 cup pretzels
- 80 g raw cashews
- 1 tsp sea salt

Preparation Instructions :

1. In a big pot of salted boiling water, cook pasta until just al dente. Drain well. Place on a tray. With a paper towel, dry. Place in a large bowl.
2. In a small bowl, combine the oil, sugar, paprika, onion, garlic, and chili powders. Pasta should get half of the mixture. Toss to coat.
3. Set the air fryer to 200C. In the air fryer basket, put the pasta. For five minutes, cook. Stir the basket. Continue to cook for a further 5–6 minutes, or until golden and crisp. Place in a large bowl.
4. Put the nuts and pretzels in a basin. Add remaining spice mixture. Coat by tossing. Put inside the air fryer basket. Cook for three minutes at 180°C. Stir the basket. Cook for a further 2 to 3 minutes, or until golden. Add to the spaghetti before the cereal. Add salt on the surface. Toss to combine. Cool completely. Serve.

Chicken tenders with crumbles Doritos

Prep: 4h 15m prep
Cook: 20 min
Serving : 4

Ingredients

- 500g chicken tenderloins, halved crossways
- 250ml buttermilk
- 170g packet Doritos Nacho Cheese corn chips
- 1 egg, lightly whisked
- 50g plain flour
- Mild salsa, to serve

Preparation Instructions :

1. Put the chicken in a dish made of glass or ceramic. Apply buttermilk on top. For 4 hours or overnight marinating, cover and put in the refrigerator.
2. Set an air fryer to 180C before using. Use baking paper to line a baking pan.
3. In a food processor, add the corn chips and process until they are roughly chopped. Place on a plate. The egg should be put in a small bowl. On a separate dish, spread out the flour.
4. Drain the chicken, discarding the buttermilk. Shake off any extra flour after dipping the chicken in it. After dipping in the egg, coat the corn chips firmly with your fingers. Put on the tray that has been prepared.
5. In the air fryer, add half the chicken, and cook for 8 to 10 minutes, or until golden and well done. The remaining chicken tenders in the same way. Put on a serving dish. Salsa is recommended.

Air Fryer Parsnips

Prep: 5 prep
Cook: 12 min
Serving : 4

Ingredients

- 4 Parsnips
- Pinch Salt and Black Pepper
- 1 tablespoon Olive Oil
- Optional Extras
- ¼ teaspoon Garlic Powder
- ½ teaspoon Dried Herbs
- 1 tablespoon Honey
- Sprinkle Thyme for garnish

Preparation Instructions :

1. Parsnips should be peeled and sliced into equal size batons.
2. Put in a big bowl and top with olive oil.
3. Add salt and black pepper to taste.
Optional : At this time, add any additional optional extra flavorings.
4. To evenly coat, combine with a spoon or your hands. Put everything in a single layer in the air fryer basket.
5. 200°C/400°F should be the temperature setting for air fry mode. Cook for 6 minutes, flip over, and then cook for an additional 6 to 8 minutes, or until crispy and golden.
6. Sprinkle some fresh thyme over top as a garnish.

Apple Turnovers

Prep: 10 prep
Cook: 10 min
Serving : 4

Ingredients

- 2 Bramley apples or 3 smaller varieties (Granny Smiths, Royal Galas)
- 2 tbsp + 1 tbsp brown sugar
- 1 tsp ground cinnamon
- 1 tbsp lemon juice
- 320g puff pastry
- 2 tbsp milk

Preparation Instructions :

1. Apples should be peeled and diced into equal pieces.
2. Combine with 1 tbsp of lemon juice, 2 tbsp of brown sugar, and 1 tsp of ground cinnamon
3. Place in air fryer basket and cook for 10 minutes at 190°C/380°F, shaking after five minutes. The apples can be stewed in a skillet on the stove if you desire a smoother filling.
4. Lay out the puff pastry on a floured board after cutting it into four equal pieces.
5. The cooked apple should be divided among each piece of dough and placed on one side, leaving a border of about 1 cm. Before folding each puff pastry over, brush some milk on the edges using a pastry brush.
6. Once all of the sides are securely attached to one another, press the edges down with a fork.
7. Pierce a hole in the top of the apple turnover and baste it with milk to release the steam.
8. Place the basket of the air fryer in each apple turnover. Spray some oil on your air fryer basket or line it with baking paper if it tends to stick.
9. Air fried for 10 to 12 minutes at the same temperature, gently turning the food over halfway through. When it's done, the puff pastry should be flaky and golden brown.

Chocolate Chip Oatmeal Cookies

Prep: 20 prep
Cook: 10 min
Serving : 4

Ingredients

- 227 g butter, softened
- 150 g packed brown sugar
- 1 teaspoon vanilla extract
- 204 g all-purpose flour
- 150 g sugar
- 2 large eggs, room temperature
- 255 g quick-cooking oats
- 1 package (96 g) instant vanilla pudding mix

- 1 teaspoon baking soda
- 256 g semisweet chocolate chips
- 1 teaspoon salt
- 128 g chopped nuts

Preparation Instructions :

1. Set air fryer to 325 degrees. Cream the butter and sugars in a big bowl for 5-7 minutes, or until they are light and creamy. Beat in eggs and vanilla after mixing.
2. Oats, flour, dry pudding mix, baking soda, and salt should all be whisked together before being gradually added to the creamed mixture. Add nuts and chocolate chips and stir.
3. Mix in the nuts and chocolate chips.
4. Using a tablespoon, drop dough onto baking sheets and gently press down. Put one in in groups. the air-fryer basket on a greased tray, separated. 8–10 minutes, or until gently browned To cool, remove to wire racks.

Potato Croquettes

Prep: 5 min
Cook: 15 min
Serving : 8

Ingredients

- 850 g Frozen potato croquette
- Salt to serve optional
- Cooking oil spray

Preparation Instructions :

1. For five minutes, preheat the Ninja foodi air fryer to 195C/385F.
2. Take the air fryer basket out and give it a gentle cooking oil spraying.
3. Croquettes should be taken out of their package and placed in a single layer in the air fryer basket. Make sure they are not too close together, although a little contact is fine.
4. Cook for 15 to 18 minutes, rotating the croquettes halfway through, until the exterior is crispy and golden brown.
5. Serve the croquettes right away with your preferred dipping sauce after removing the basket from the air fryer.

Crab cake

Prep: 20 min
Cook: 10 min
Serving : 4

Ingredients

- 453g crab meat, shredded
- 4 tablespoons bread crumbs

- 2 teaspoon dried parsley
- 1/2 teaspoon black pepper
- 2 tablespoon mayonnaise
- 1 teaspoon salt
- 1 large egg
- 1 teaspoon dry mustard

Preparation Instructions :

1. Start by combining the crabmeat, bread crumbs, parsley, salt, pepper, egg, mayonnaise, and dry mustard in a medium-sized mixing bowl.
2. All of the ingredients should be thoroughly combined; add additional bread crumbs if necessary, up to 2 tablespoons. This mixture should be able to be formed into patties.
3. Spray either the air fryer tray or the basket.
4. Put the crab cakes in the basket or on the baking sheet.
5. For 5 minutes, set the air fryer temperature to 400 degrees Fahrenheit.
6. Flip the food after five minutes, then air fried it for an additional five. Take out of the air fryer basket or oven.
7. For a fantastic crab cake slider, I also included a slider roll, chopped tomato, lettuce, and pre-made Remoulade sauce.

Jalapeño Poppers

Prep: 10 min
Cook: 8 min
Serving : 10 poppers

Ingredients

- 5 medium jalapeños, fresh
- 43g sharp cheddar cheese, shredded
- ½ tsp garlic powder
- ⅛ tsp black pepper
- 1 tbsp butter, melted
- 113g cream cheese, softened
- 2 tbsp green onions, chopped
- ¼ tsp salt
- 21g Panko breadcrumbs

Preparation Instructions :

1. When cutting the jalapenos in half lengthwise, wear gloves or take extra care. To completely empty the jalapeo halves of seeds and membranes, use a tiny spoon. Set aside.
2. Mix the cream cheese, sharp cheddar cheese, green onions, garlic powder, salt, and black pepper in a small bowl until well blended. Put roughly 1 tablespoon of the mixture inside each pepper.
3. Melted butter and panko breadcrumbs should be combined in a separate small dish and mixed to evenly distribute the butter among the crumbs. Spread the crumbs evenly over the cream cheese portion of the pepper.
4. Peppers should be evenly layered in the air fryer and cooked at 375 degrees F. five to eight minutes.

French onion chicken pastries

Prep: 10 min

Cook: 40 min

makes : 24

Ingredients

- 200g bacon, finely chopped
- 60g plain flour
- 200g ctn sour cream
- 1/2 x 35g pkt French onion soup mix
- 6 sheets frozen puff pastry, just thawed
- 60g butter
- 375ml salt-reduced chicken stock
- 400g chopped barbecue chicken
- 1 tbsp chopped fresh chives
- 1 egg, lightly whisked

Preparation Instructions :

1. Heat a large frying pan to a medium-high temperature. Cook the bacon for two to three minutes, or until browned. Include the butter. until dissolved, cook while stirring. Add the flour. Add chicken stock and bring to a boil after stirring. Add the chicken, French onion soup mix, chives, and sour cream. Get rid of the heat. Put in the refrigerator to chill.
2. Cut each pastry sheet into four squares. In the center of each square, place 2 tbsp of the chicken mixture. Along the long sides of the filling, cut the pastry diagonally into three strips of equal width. Fold the filling's short ends over. A pastry strip should be folded over the filling. Another strip should be folded in, barely overlapping the first strip. Alternate strips over filling until completely enclosed. Brush with egg .
3. n the Ninja foodi air fryer basket, place six pastries. 190°C air frying for ten minutes. The remaining pastries should be repeated.

Cheeseburger Stuffed Biscuits

Prep: 20 min

Cook: 7 min

Serves : 8

Ingredients

- 453g lean ground beef
- 1 teaspoon Worcestershire sauce
- 16 dill pickle chips, blotted dry with paper towels
- 1/4 teaspoon black pepper
- 1 teaspoon sesame seeds
- 255g ketchup
- 1 tablespoon sweet pickle relish
- 1/2 medium yellow or sweet onion, diced
- 4 slices American cheese
- 1/2 teaspoon salt
- 1 tube GRANDS refrigerated biscuits
- For Burger Sauce :
- 85g mayonnaise

Preparation Instructions :

1. In a large nonstick pan, cook the ground beef and crumble it. Add the onion after it is approximately halfway done cooking. Add the Worcestershire sauce, salt, and pepper once there are no more picks remaining. Cool down.
2. Divide each biscuit in half. Each piece is slightly stretched. On half of the biscuit rounds, heap a few teaspoons of the ground beef mixture.
3. Top each mound of ground beef with two pickle slices and half a slice of cheese. Put a half of a biscuit on top of each. While pressing firmly on the seams, stretch as necessary to seal the edges.
4. Spray the tops of the biscuits gently with cooking spray and sprinkle with sesame seeds.
5. Spray a little oil on the air fryer basket. At a time, prepare 4 filled biscuits.
6. For seven to eight minutes, air fry at 350 degrees. At around six minutes, check. When the biscuits are golden, they are finished.
7. In a small bowl, combine the ingredients for the burger sauce.
8. Serve burger sauce beside the stuffed biscuits.

Ham and Cheese Biscuit Sandwiches

Prep: 10 min
Cook: 10 min
Serves : 8

Ingredients

- 1 package Grand Biscuits
- 1/4 pound sliced deli ham
- 1/4 pound sliced Swiss cheese
- 1/4 cup honey mustard dressing
- 2 tablespoons melted butter
- 2 tablespoon honey

Preparation Instructions :

1. The biscuit should be split in half using your hands. About one teaspoon of honey mustard dressing should be spread on the bottom layer before some Swiss cheese slices are added. Add two to three slices of ham after that.
2. Apply cooking spray on your basket. Melted butter should be brushed on top of the biscuits. Set the air fryer to the air fryer setting and cook the food for 6 to 8 minutes, turning halfway through. Just before serving, drizzle with honey.

Ham Wtth Honey Brown Sugar Glaze

Prep: 5 min
Cook: 55 min
Serves : 10

Ingredients

- 9-1.36 kg boneless, fully cooked ham
- 110 g brown sugar
- 1.25 ml Cinnamon
- 60 ml orange juice (or 1 orange juiced)
- black pepper , to taste
- BROWN SUGAR GLAZE INGREDIENTS
- 85 g honey
- 1.25 ml Clove (optional)
- 30 ml mustard (optional) or apple cider vinegar

Preparation Instructions :

1. Before cooking, take the ham out of the fridge and let it sit at room temperature for about 2 hours.
2. Brown sugar, honey, orange juice, optional mustard, cinnamon, clove (optional), and black pepper are all combined to make the brown sugar glaze. Brown sugar will melt and glaze will be well blended as you heat and whisk. Place aside.
3. The ham should be free of the netting. If the ham is not pre-sliced, score it with shallow criss-cross slices of 1/2 inch.
4. Two long, overlapping foil sheets should be used to line the ninja foodi air fryer basket. Brush about a third of the glaze over the ham after placing it on top of the foil. Ham is covered with foil, which is then securely wrapped.
5. Put the ham in an air fryer. Apply a little of the glaze, then securely cover the ham in foil.
6. Air fry for 25 minutes at 340 °F. After gently removing the foil from the air fryer basket, apply additional glaze onto the ham (make sure to reserve some glaze for finishing & serving). Once more, Air Fry for 25 minutes at 340° by sealing the foil securely.
7. If utilizing the basket-style air fryer method, open up the foil once again after the 50 minutes of cooking, and now press the foil down around the edges of the ham. With the foil, make a boat that catches the fluids and prevents the ham from drying out. Simply take off the foil from the pan when utilizing the Oven Style Air Fryer technique.
8. In order to get the desired level of caramelization, increase heat to Air Fry at 360°F for 5 minutes and brush on a little extra glaze. Before serving, let the ham rest for 5 minutes.

Whole Chicken - Rotisserie Style

Prep: 5 min

Cook: 1 hr
Serves : 6

Ingredients

- 9-1.36 kg boneless, fully cooked ham
- 1 Whole chicken, removed giblets
- 15 grams Kosher Salt
- 15 grams Garlic powder
- 2 grams Dried basil
- 2 grams Dried thyme

- BROWN SUGAR GLAZE INGREDIENTS
- 28.3 grams avocado oil
- 15 grams Freshly ground black pepper
- 15 grams Paprika (I prefer smoked paprika)
- 2 grams Dried oregano

Preparation Instructions :

1. Spread a paste made from the oil and all of the ingredients over the chicken.
2. Spray cooking oil on the air fryer basket. Cook the chicken for 50 minutes at 360°F with the breast side down in the basket. Cook the chicken for 10 more minutes with the breast side facing up.
3. Make sure the internal temperature of the breast flesh is 165°F. Carve, then serve.

Air fryer Turkey with gravy

Prep: 10 min
Cook: 3 HRS 15 MINS
Serves : 12

Ingredients

- 6.35 kg raw Whole Turkey
- 4 cloves garlic , sliced thin
- black pepper , to taste
- 360 ml chicken broth

- 90 g butter , cut into slices
- 15 ml kosher salt , or to taste
- Oil , to coat turkey
- 95 g flour (for the gravy)

Preparation Instructions :

1. Take off the turkey's neck bones and giblet. Pat the turkey dry.
2. Insert the garlic cloves and slices of butter between the skin and the turkey breasts. Salt and pepper the turkey after seasoning it with oil.
3. Spray oil into the air fryer and insert the lower rack. Put the turkey in the air fryer breast side down. Over the turkey, pour 1/2 cup of the broth. Put the air fryer's cover and extender ring on it.
4. For around 2 1/2 to 3 hours, air fry at 350°F.
5. Baste with chicken broth every 30 minutes (the first 2 bastes will be with the remaining broth. After that, baste from the broth & juices at the bottom of the air fryer).
6. Remove the air fryer cover and extender ring after cooking for two hours. Reposition the turkey in the air fryer by lifting it out, turning it breast side up, and doing so. Place the extender ring and cover back on the turkey and continue cooking it until the internal

temperature of the thickest parts of the thigh, wings, and breast reaches 165°F and the juices flow clear when you cut between the leg and thigh (about 30 minutes – 1 hour).

7. Allow to rest for 15 to 20 minutes.

8. Make the gravy while the turkey is resting. From the air fryer, remove the bottom rack. Skim the pieces from the soup and drippings, leaving the turkey juices in the air fryer.

9. In a medium bowl, place the flour. About 1 cup of the drippings and broth should be added to the flour, and it should be mixed until smooth. Add the remaining drippings and broth to the air fryer along with the flour mixture. until smooth, whisk.

10. Put the lid back on the air fryer and cook the food for 10 minutes at 400°F, or until it thickens, while whisking a couple of times.

Sunday Roast with Classic Roast Potatoes

Prep: 10 min
Cook: 16-18 mins
Serves : 6

Ingredients

- 1 tbsp loosely packed fresh rosemary leaves
- 1/2 – 1 tbsp olive oil
- 1–2 tbsp unsalted butter
- kosher salt
- 1 tsp black or pink peppercorns
- 1–1.4 kg eye of round roast
- classic roast potatoes
- HORSERADISH CREAM INGREDIENTS
- 70 g sour cream
- 1 1/2 tbsp prepared horseradish
- kosher salt
- 1 tbsp honey

Preparation Instructions :

1. Grind the rosemary, 1 1/2 teaspoons salt, and the peppercorns in a mortar and pestle or in a small bowl using the handle of a wooden spoon. It should be a thick mixture. With paper towels, pat the roast to dry. Depending on the size of the roast, rub 1/2 to 1 tablespoon of oil all over the meat before seasoning it on all sides.

2. Spray canola oil on the Ninja foodi air fryer basket. Put the roast in the basket's middle. Attach the air fryer cover after placing the basket within the pot. Press the Air Fry button and adjust the cooking temperature to 325°F (165°C) for 16 to 18 minutes per kilogram of beef (start with the lower amount of time and add more time if needed).

3. Make the horseradish cream in the meantime by combining the sour cream, horseradish, and

1/4 teaspoon salt in a small bowl. Salt the dish to taste and correct the seasoning. When not in use, cover and place in the fridge.

4. When the specified cooking time has passed, place an instant-read thermometer into the center of the meat; for medium, the reading should be between 135 and 145 degrees Fahrenheit (57 and 63 degrees Celsius). If the roast is not done to your liking, continue cooking it for an additional 2 minutes at a time. The roast should be moved to a chopping board using tongs. Depending on the size of the roast, place 1-2 teaspoons of butter on top and let it to melt. Drizzle with the honey, loosely cover with foil, and allow to rest for 15 to 20 minutes.

5. Cook the potatoes while the meat rests. Serve the potatoes and horseradish cream with the roast, which has been cut into thin, round slices.

Duo Crisp + Air Fryer Cheesy Beef and Rice Casserole

Prep: 10 min

Cook: 16-18 mins

Serves : 6

Ingredients

- 450g ground beef
- 128g frozen peas (or other frozen vegetable or double the carrots)
- 304g condensed cream of mushroom soup canned or homemade
- 425g beef broth
- 128g uncooked long grain rice rinsed
- 128g chopped carrots
- 128g shredded Cheddar cheese

Preparation Instructions :

1. Place ground beef in the pressure cooker. Select the SAUTE feature on the display panel, set the volume to HIGH, then press START. Stop after browning the meat until no pink is visible.

2. Remove fat. Browned meat should be transferred to a shallow dish and loosely covered with foil.

3. Deglaze the pan by adding broth and scraping the brown pieces from the bottom with a wooden spoon. Stir in the rice that has been washed.

4. In that order, add the soup, cooked meat, and veggies to the pot. Keep still. Lock the lid of the pressure cooker.

5. Make your selection for the PRESSURE COOK function on the display screen. Select START after modifying the timer to 15 minutes.

6. Allow the pressure to naturally release for ten minutes after the allotted time has passed, then quickly remove the remaining pressure. After combining the ingredients, level the top and sprinkle an even layer of cheese on top.

7. Add in the air fryer and Set the timer 5 minutes and the temperature to 400°F.

8. Remove the cover and drop the cheese on the protecting pad once it has melted completely and started to brown. Serve heated after spreading into individual bowls.

Beef Fried Rice

Prep: 10 min
Cook: 20 mins
Serves : 6

Ingredients

- 226g Skirt Steak sliced against the grain
- 340g White Onion Diced
- 21g Carrots Diced
- Coconut Oil Cooking Spray or Olive Oil Cooking Spray
- 2 Great Day Farms Hard-Boiled Eggs
- 4 Cups Cold Cooked White Rice
- 21g Celery Diced
- 4-6 Tbsp Soy Sauce or Gluten Free Soy Sauce

Preparation Instructions :

1. The steak should be cut, then placed in the air fryer basket. Cook for five minutes at 390 degrees.
2. After flipping, cook for a further five minutes.
3. Use foil to line the air fryer basket. To ensure that air may still flow, make sure not to completely cover the basket. Most of the time, I roll it up on the side.
4. Apply coconut oil or olive oil spray on the foil. Place each item in the basket over the foil in the proper sequence.
5. Add a generous layer of coconut oil spray to the top of the mixture after stirring to combine.
6. Cook for five minutes in the air fryer at 390°.
7. Open the container with care and toss the rice and mixture once more, adding more soy sauce or spray if necessary.
8. Add the sliced or chopped hard-boiled eggs by stirring.
9. Cooking time is extended by 3 minutes at 390. Stir, then plate.

Air fryer chocolate chip pudding

Prep: 10 min
Cook: 15 mins
Serves : 6

Ingredients

- 256 bread cubed
- 50g sugar
- 32g chocolate chips

- 1 egg
- 227g heavy cream
- 1/2 tsp vanilla extract

Preparation Instructions :

1. Apply cooking spray to the interior of a baking dish that will fit inside the ninja foodi air fryer.
2. Bread cubes should be placed in a baking dish. Sprinkle whatever chocolate chips you're using on top of the bread.
3. Combine the egg, whipped cream, vanilla, and sugar in a separate bowl. After adding the egg mixture to the bread cubes, wait for five minutes.
4. In the air fryer basket, place the baking pan. Cook the bread pudding in the air fryer at 350F for 15 minutes, or until it is well heated through.

Air Fryer Spicy Lamb

Prep: 10 min
Cook: 10 mins
Serves : 6

Ingredients

- 900g Boneless Lamb Shoulder (Cut Into 1 Inch Thick Piece strips)
- 29ml Shaoxing Wine
- Spice Mix
- 28g Cumin Powder
- 1 Tablespoon Ground Red Chili, Red Pepper Flakes Or Cayenne Pepper
- 15g White Sesame Seed
- 15g Ground Funnel
- 15g Himalayan Salt
- 15g Ground Ginger
- 15g Ground Garlic
- 15g Cumin Seeds
- 5g Sichuan Peppercorns
- Fresh Cilantro For Garnish

Preparation Instructions :

1. Combine all the ground spices with any optional cooking wine in a large mixing bowl. After that, you may choose whether to marinate or not. The lamb will taste less chewy after being marinated.
2. The lamb strips should be mixed well with 1/4 of your spice mixture before marinating. If you're not going to marinate, add the lamb strips in sliced form to the big basin and well mix. Then set it into a basket for an air fryer.
3. Once your air basket is full, air fried it for 10 to 15 minutes at 350°F, or until golden and crispy. To ensure that the lamb pieces are air fried evenly, flip them over or give the air basket a thorough shake halfway through. Place some freshly bedded cilantro on top of it once it has finished cooking. Sesame and cumin seeds should be added on top. Serve hot for the tastiest results.

Cajun Shrimp Pasta

Prep: 5 min
Cook: 15 mins
Serves : 6

Ingredients

- 250 g of your favorite type of pasta
- 450g of raw shrimp (deveined, cleaned, and tails removed)
- 2 tablespoons of cajun seasoning
- 1 tablespoon of olive oil
- 1 tablespoon of butter
- 60ml of dry white wine (optional)
- 340g of heavy cream
- 43g of fresh finely grated Parmesan Cheese
- salt for pasta water
- salt and pepper to taste

Preparation Instructions :

1. Bring water and salt to a boil in a pot. Cook the pasta until it is al dente, or tender but still firm. Pasta should be drained and set aside.
2. Melted butter, extra virgin olive oil, and cajun spice have to be mixed in a small bowl. While the air fryer is heating up, let the food marinade.
3. Set the air fryer to 360 degrees of heating. Once prepared, fry the shrimp for 8–10 minutes in a single layer. The shrimp don't require turning. When it's finished, take it out of the air fryer and and set it aside.
4. The skillet should be heated to medium-high. In a single layer, add the shrimp to the skillet with the marinade.
5. Cook until golden brown, then turn and cook the other side. Usually requires a similar length of time as an air fryer.
6. Now take a skillet and, if using wine, add heavy cream to it. Use the same skillet you used to cook the shrimp on the stove. Observe the cream bubble. Add the cheese after lowering the heat slightly. The cheese should melt.
7. The cooked pasta and the shrimp should be added. To coat, stir. Add some of the pasta water to the sauce if it needs to be thinned. Sprinkle on parsley at the end and more Parmesan cheese.

Air fryer spiral fries

Prep: 5 min
Cook: 22 mins

Serves : 6

Ingredients

- 3 Potatoes, (medium sized)
- 3-5 cloves Garlic, minced **
- 2 Tbsp. Olive Oil
- 1/2 tsp. sea salt or kosher salt

Preparation Instructions :

1. Prepare potatoes using a spiralizer.
2. Spiralize some potatoes and add some olive oil to the air fryer's basket.
3. Prepare for two minutes at 350 degrees.
4. Use tongs to "toss" the potatoes, spreading the olive oil evenly and moving them about to ensure even cooking.
5. 8 minutes into cooking, "toss" once again.
6. Cook for another 8 minutes after adding the minced garlic.
7. Cook for a further 4 minutes if necessary after "tossing" once more. How crisp you prefer your fries will determine how long they need to fry.
8. Serve immediately.

Air fryer beef Stew

Cook: 25 mins
Serves : 6-8

Ingredients

- 1kg beef chunks
- 2 large carrots
- 1/2 tsp black pepper
- 2-4 tbsp worcestershire sauce
- 4 large potatoes diced
- 1lt beef stock
- 1/2 tsp smoked paprika
- Fresh thyme

Preparation Instructions :

1. All of the dry ingredients should be added to the Ninja foodi pot . Add the wet ingredients and well whisk or combine.
2. Set the timer for 25 minutes and cook the beef.
3. After finishing, be sure to vent gradually to avoid getting a lot of soup all over your kitchen.
4. Meat, potatoes, and carrots break apart and are simple, mildly spiced, and tasty.

Air fryer Meatloaf Shepherd's Pie

Prep: 20 min
Cook: 60 mins
Serves : 6-8

Ingredients

- 2 tablespoons unsalted butter
- 4 cloves garlic, minced
- 250 g crumbled leftover meatloaf
- 340ml beef broth
- 2 tablespoons mustard
- 1 teaspoon dried marjoram or oregano
- Freshly ground black pepper, to taste
- 128g frozen peas
- 28g cup grated Parmesan cheese
- 1 medium onion, coarsely chopped
- 1 cup frozen sliced carrots
- 2 tablespoons all-purpose flour
- 170g ketchup
- 1 tablespoon Worcestershire sauce
- Salt, to taste
- 500g package precooked mashed potatoes
- 113g sour cream

Preparation Instructions :

1. Preheat the air frier to 375 F. In a large skillet, melt the butter over medium heat.
2. Add the onion and garlic and sauté for 4 to 5 minutes, or until the onions are turning translucent.
3. Add the carrots and sauté for 4 minutes, or until the carrots thaw.
4. Add the crumbled meatloaf and sauté for 4 to 5 minutes longer until the mixture is hot and combined. Add the flour and sauté for 3 more minutes.
5. Add the broth, ketchup, mustard, Worcestershire sauce, marjoram, and salt and pepper to taste. Stir. Simmer the mixture for 10 minutes, stirring occasionally.
6. Meanwhile, heat the refrigerated potatoes as directed on the package, or use leftover mashed potatoes, if available.
7. Add the peas and sour cream to the beef mixture in the skillet and stir to combine.
8. Pour into a 2 1/2-quart casserole dish and spread the mixture level.
9. Top with the mashed potatoes and spread to cover, then run a fork over the potatoes to make small peaks that will brown in the air fryer. Sprinkle with the Parmesan cheese.
10. Air fried the shepherd's pie for 25 to 35 minutes or until the filling is bubbly and the potatoes are golden brown on top. Let cool for 10 minutes before serving.

Beef Tips

Prep: 2 min
Cook: 12 min
Serves : 6

Ingredients

- 900g ribeye or New York steak, cut into 1-inch cubes
- 16.8g sea salt
- 8g garlic powder
- 8g paprika
- 16g coconut aminos
- 8g black pepper
- 16g onion powder
- 16g rosemary crushed

Preparation Instructions :

1. Steak cubes should be placed in a medium bowl.
2. Combine the salt, pepper, paprika, onion, garlic, and rosemary in a small bowl. Mix thoroughly.
3. On the steak cubes, generously sprinkle the mixed dry spice. To spread the seasoning equally, stir.
4. The steak has been season with the coconut aminos. Mix thoroughly.
5. Give it five minutes to sit.
6. Put the steak in the air fryer basket in a single layer.
7. Cook for 12 minutes at 380F. To ensure that the steak cooks evenly, shake the basket halfway through.
8. Before serving, take it out of the air fryer and let it cool for a while.

Air fryer Vegetable stir fry

Prep: 2 min
Cook: 12 min
Serves : 6

Ingredients

- 200 grams extra firm tofu, cut into strips (about 1 cup)
- 15 stalks asparagus, ends trimmed and cut in half
- 12 brussels sprouts, halved
- 9 brown mushrooms, sliced
- 4 cloves garlic, minced
- 2 teaspoon Italiano seasoning
- 1 teaspoon sesame oil (or olive oil)
- 1\2 teaspoon soy sauce
- salt and pepper, to taste
- roasted white sesame seeds (for garnish)

Preparation Instructions :

1. Toss all the ingredients together in a large mixing bowl.
2. Depending on how well done you want the veggies, transfer to an air fryer basket and air fry at 350 F for 7-8 minutes.
3. Shake the basket once more in the middle.
4. Serve with a serving of steamed rice after being removed from the air fryer basket and sprinkled with toasted white sesame seeds.

Printed in Great Britain
by Amazon

17239790R00047